Around the House In Eighty Days

Shirley Cook

HARVEST HOUSE PUBLISHERS
Irvine, California 92714

AROUND THE HOUSE IN EIGHTY DAYS

Copyright © 1980 by Harvest House Publishers
Irvine, California 92714

Library of Congress Catalog Card Number 80-80091
ISBN 0-89081-220-9

Printed in the United States of America.

CONTENTS

❖

ORDINARY THINGS

"If only I didn't have to stay home and take care of the children, I'd find real fulfillment in the business world."

"I wish I didn't have to get up and go to work every day; I'd be so happy staying home."

Whatever our circumstances, most of us imagine that, under *different* circumstances, we would really shine! Our ordinary, everyday tasks get us down from time to time.

I've often had "cabin fever" as I stayed home day after day caring for children who came down with stomach flu, one by one. I remember praying, "Oh, God, I'd be a much better Christian if only. . . ."

But I've learned a better way—better than complaining about my duties as a wife and mother, better than wishing I could start over and somehow arrange my own destiny. I've learned to see *the hand of God* in my own surroundings—and you can, too, if you just look!

Jesus often spoke in parables (earthly stories with heavenly meanings), and I believe He is still speaking through the common things and events we encounter each day. If you and I will only open our spiritual eyes and see God's parables, we will be fulfilled—filled full of God's blessings.

> I looked for Thee in visions
> And raptures of delight.
> I thought I'd feel emotion
> And maybe see the "light."

Forgive me, Lord, for seeking "it"
Instead of seeing Thee
In all the ordinary things
That daily compass me.

I'll go through each day praising,
For Thou art everywhere,
And all my common tasks, Lord,
Are sanctified by prayer.

"What God has cleansed, do not call common or ordinary" (Acts 10:15b).

TOYS

Phyllis had planned a visit from Santa Claus, complete with sleigh and a bag of toys, for her four-year-old. He was to arrive Christmas morning after the rest of the family had gathered for breakfast.

An eight-year-old cousin was dubious about the expected visit, and proclaimed in an authoritative voice, "There's no such thing as Santa Claus—and I know it!"

Upon hearing the jingle of bells outside, both boys pressed their noses to the window, then turned in awed wonder as Santa bounded into the room with rosy cheeks, twinkling eyes, and all the rest.

Long after the toys were distributed and Santa had left, the eight-year-old, who never uttered a word during the entire visit, continued to stare out the window. Finally, turning to his aunt, he exclaimed in his most serious voice, "Well, I'm not sure about Santa Claus, but I'll tell you one thing—I don't believe in the tooth fairy."

To a child, seeing is believing. And how often well-educated, mature adults give the same worn-out excuse for not believing the good news of the gospel: "Well, if I could see a miracle, then maybe I'd believe."

Jesus taught that *believing is seeing.* He once told the story of a rich man who through unbelief went to hell. He looked across the darkness and saw Lazarus, a poor beggar who, though he had no earthly riches, by faith had now arrived in paradise. The rich man begged Lazarus to tell his brothers the way of salvation. He said that if Lazarus arose from the dead, his

9

brothers would surely believe. But Lazarus did not go, for "neither will they be persuaded, though one rose from the dead."

How true. Jesus rose from the dead, yet many still do not believe. Do you? Do you believe that Jesus died and rose for you? Do you believe that He is able to do exceedingly abundantly above all that you can ask or think?

"Blessed are those who have not seen, and yet have believed" (John 20:29b).

Today's Scripture: Ecclesiastes 2:4-11

BUBBLES

"Oh, I just love it!" I squealed. "It's something I've always wanted." Several times during the following years I repeated the words, "I love it, and absolutely could not get along without it." Then I found that I could.

My automatic dishwasher broke. My husband tried to fix it, but it had sizzled and sighed its last breath. "Well, I'll just have to get another one, and the sooner the better."

"No," he said. "There are other things we need more than a dishwasher right now."

He was right. Becky needed braces on her teeth,

and Kathy had another year of college—so back to the old dishpan. My bubble had burst!

As I stood washing dishes one day, I suddenly realized how good the warm water felt splashing over my hands. The clean, soapy fragrance steaming up into my nostrils reminded me of when, as a child, I had stood on an old tin-can stool while Mother washed and I dried, and we laughed, sang, and told each other stories. It had been fun washing dishes then.

I ruffled the water and watched a bubble rise in the air, its liquid rainbows shimmering in the light of the kitchen window. A slight touch of my finger zapped it (and my memories) away like magic.

It reminded me of the bubbles I think I need to keep me happy, like my automatic dishwasher. Do I place too much importance on *things?*

Things are transitory joys. How fleeting! How likely to pop and disappear! The Bible instructs us to hold lightly onto physical life itself, for we have no control of the future. We're rather to hold fast to those things of eternal value—the laws of nature, the lessons of life, the love of God. Such things cannot be zapped away.

"What is your life! It is a vapor that appears for a little while and then vanishes away" (James 4:14b).

MENDING

"Honey, where's my cashmere sweater?" my husband asked. "You know—I asked you to mend a hole in it."

"Mom, I can't find my jeans anywhere. I remember you said you wanted to shorten them, but where are they?"

The answer always comes back the same. "Have you looked in the back of my closet? I have a few things stacked up that need mending."

A few things? If the stack gets any higher. . . . Pity the person who sees his or her "lost" garment near the bottom of the pile!

I hate to mend, but I seem to get a constant flow of missing buttons and ripped seams. Oh, I occasionally enjoy constructing a dress, knitting an afghan, or even embroidering a pillow—but mend a tear? It seems so insignificant.

Fashion-modeling a new dress in front of my husband gets more glory than pointing out my tailoring abilities on a reattached pocket. (But now that I think about it, I'm sure he'd be delighted to see some of those long-forgotten clothes hanging in his closet again!)

I can't really forget the clothes to be mended. They haunt me. I know they're in the dark, hoping I'll notice and begin patching some rips and tears to give them a new lease on life.

I can think of some relationships that need mending, too: a thoughtless word, almost forgotten; a broken spirit that could use encouragement; a neglected person thrown back into a dark corner of

12

life, just waiting for a smile—a touch of friendship. It's easy to ignore these quiet, unassuming people who are no longer involved in the rush of activity.

They sit behind drawn drapes, in rest homes, on hospital beds. Some have been abandoned by their mates or their children. The list grows longer and longer. I keep looking the other way. There's no glory in a darkened house where an old wrinkled woman sheds tears. I want to be where the action is!

But God loves to mend hearts. He cares. He is looking for some willing needles and thread to go and put together these lonely, torn lives. Am I willing to be made willing?

"He has sent me to bind up the brokenhearted" (Isaiah 61:1b).

Today's Scripture: Hebrews 11:23-28

BLUEBERRY PIE

"What is it?"

"What do you mean, 'What is it?' It's your favorite—blueberry pie."

"Oh, yeah," my husband drawled, "but where are the blueberries?"

Snuggled between thick layers of crust was a thin purple line. You couldn't even see the blueberries, much less taste them. I guess I should have used the whole can.

It was my first pie. That was a long time ago (28 years, to be exact), and if I were easily discouraged, it could have been my last. But I knew that my young husband loved pies (his mother made the greatest, he said), and here was a challenge. I would learn to make good pies too—if it killed him!

Today, after many failures, "I've often overheard him say, "Wait till you taste my wife's pies—they're the greatest!"

What made me keep baking? Love. I love him and want to please him, so I didn't give up on pie-baking or those countless other details that go into making a happy husband (and wife).

So why is it so easy to give up when I fail as a Christian? If I lose my temper and blurt out unkind words, I often excuse myself with, "I can't help it—that's just my nature." Or when asked to give a speech and my knees turn to jelly, isn't it only right to say no, because it scares me to death?

The love of Christ constrains me. Surely the desire to please and honor Him will challenge me to trust Him for victory over such sins (yes, sins) as anger and fear. It's no "piece of pie" to serve the Lord, but trusting Him is a "peaceable fruit."

"Therefore, my beloved brethren, be steadfast, unmovable, always abounding in the work of the Lord, for you know that your labor is not in vain in the Lord" (1 Corinthians 15:58).

Today's Scripture: Psalm 1

PLANTS

I love house plants, and after spending the day at

Sherri's I decided I'd also bring the outdoors inside. I set the plants in pots, on stands, and dangling from macrame hangers. When my husband walked in the door that evening, he called out, "Hey, either send me a safari guide or pass the machete."

Well, maybe I did overdo it a bit, but time took care of my trial at greenhousewifery. The plants all died or are in the process of dying! There's still a split-leaf philodendron that split down the middle, a spider plant that has crawled back into its web, and an asparagus fern that looks like it's ready for hollandaise sauce.

I don't know what I did wrong. The books said that if the plants get too much water, they'll turn yellow;

GREEN IS BEAUTIFUL

if too little, they'll turn brown. Nothing was said about black or white leaves.

There were also instructions about light: but the same room that's filtered in the morning is brilliant in the afternoon! I wore myself out moving plants around the house all day.

The growth of all life depends a great deal on the proper amount of water and light. Even our spiritual lives will dry out and curl up if not properly cared for. And as parents, we're also responsible for the tender young ones in our care.

The Bible speaks of the Word of God as water and Jesus Christ as the Light of the world. As we satisfy our thirst with God's Word and walk in the Light as He is in the Light, we'll not only grow, but we'll enjoy a continuous fellowship with God. And that's what I covet for my children, too.

Let your loved ones see you walk with Jesus today. Water their parched spirits with the Word of God— and then watch them grow!

"Those that are planted in the house of the Lord shall flourish in the courts of our God" (Psalm 92:13).

Today's Scripture: 1 John 1:6-10

CAVITIES

"But, Mom, I brush my teeth so good. Why do I have to go to the dentist?"

"I think I see a tiny cavity, Honey. Let's get it filled before it gets any bigger."

My daughter clamped her jaws tight as a tear oozed out from under her lashes.

I patted her shoulder. "It won't hurt. It's only a little cavity."

"Well," she brightened, "if it's only a little one, maybe I could just brush longer and harder, and it'll go away."

"I'm afraid not, Sweetie."

"But we could just forget about it and. . . ."

How like a child to handle problems that way! Forget it and maybe it'll go away. But I must admit, I've done the same thing, and found the problems growing instead of disappearing. Or in trying to cover up by self-effort, I've magnified them beyond repair.

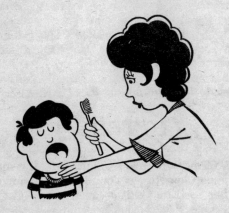

There are many things that we can and must handle ourselves, especially in our relationships with others; but in the matter of personal sin, no amount of self-effort or wishing it away will help.

I tried for years to justify myself before God. I went

17

to church. I was baptized. I prayed. Then I decided that if I could just forget about God, maybe my sins would go away.

But it wasn't until I took my sin to the only One who could do anything about it that I was cleansed and made whole. Jesus Christ is the only Savior from sin—those past sins, the ones I commit today, and the ones tomorrow. If I want to be mature about it, I'll bring my sin to Him now, before it grows, that He may do His work of cleansing and filling.

"If we confess our sins, He is faithful and just to forgive us our sins and to cleanse us from all unrighteousness" (1 John 1:9).

Today's Scripture: Philippians 1:1-11

LETTERS

I have a friend who has a unique gift. She makes you feel good! Sometimes, completely unknown to her, she has used her gift at exactly the right moment.

Example:

"Ding-a-ling-a-ling."

"Hello."

"Hello, beautiful," says her happy voice. "I just called to tell you I love you."

"Well, thank you," I say, suddenly feeling lighthearted.

"Thank you for being you," she adds before hanging up.

The day that had started as a disaster (I burned my husband's toast and broke his egg yoke) took a sharp turn down the road of delight. I was loved. She had given me a fresh love to share with others. My family looked beautiful to me, and the meeting with the school principal didn't seem so dreadful now.

This same friend sends cheery letters, sprinkled liberally with words of encouragement and love. I'm always excited to open a letter from her. She doesn't gossip or run down the pastor. She doesn't complain about the weather or her husband's faults.

She's a breath of fresh air in a sometimes-stale world. It isn't because she's had an easy life, either. She's had more than her share of heartache and grief, but she's found that the trials of life can either make her "bitter" or "better," depending on her reactions to them.

She has found a better way. She sees God in her circumstances and thanks Him, and in turn her life has become a blessing and encouragement to others.

She not only sends letters of hope and cheer to others, but she *is* a letter of hope and cheer.

Are you?

Am I?

"You are shown to be the epistle of Christ ministered by us, written not with ink, but with the Spirit of the living God; not in tables of stone, but in fleshy tables of the heart" (2 Corinthians 3:3).

19

BOXES

"After I open this one, I'll know what's in this one too," Barby said, holding up two identically wrapped gift boxes. The little girls who were gathered around the "Birthday girl" snickered and jabbed each other. "Don't be too sure," Stacey said. "Just 'cause they look the same on the outside doesn't mean they're the same inside."

She was right. The red-and-white-striped, hexagonal boxes contained completely different surprises—a stuffed animal, and three pairs of Snoopy socks.

As I looked around at the wiggling, hopping girls, I thought they looked alike too. Shiny hair in barrettes, a missing tooth or two, and the same strange sounds emitted from each one—like a pen of piglets. Yet I knew that each of these girls was different inside, with private hopes and fears. Perhaps they were afraid to voice their true feelings, afraid to be different.

This fear continues into adulthood, boxing us in. It inhibits us from being the whole, complete original creations God intended us to be. Of course, we have similarities that bring us together in common bonds of interest, but it's easy to lose sight of our own individuality. The pressure is on to conform. Dress like this. Drive that car. Live in this neighborhood.

We do need a pattern, but we don't need a box. Jesus said to follow Him. He is our pattern. He is our

Life. He is our freedom. If He makes us free, we are free indeed.

By faith leap out of that box of conformity today. Look unto Jesus. Live in His Word. You can't keep life in a box.

"With men this is impossible, but with God all things are possible" (Matthew 19:26).

Today's Scripture: 2 Corinthians 1:3-6

OLD SLIPPERS

"No, I don't want to throw them away," Opa said, his German chin hard and square. "I like these slippers even if they are old and full of holes. They're comfortable and warm—like old friends."

Those old slippers. Mimi (she doesn't like to be called Grandma) bought him a new pair for Christmas, but will he wear them? You'd think she was trying to replace one of his grandchildren or something.

"Just look," said my children's grandfather, turning his foot this way and that, "it's molded to my foot."

"It's just plain moldy, if you ask me," Mimi mumbled.

"I didn't ask you," he grinned. "Don't you have something that's old and comfortable that you don't want to give up?"

"Well, yes," she laughed, "you!"

Grandparents! They're priceless.

We all get attached to things, especially if they give us warmth and comfort. And evidently Opa's slippers do. I like my warm, furry ones too.

Warmth and comfort. That's what everyone wants. But slippers give only temporary comfort, because eventually we have to get back into our work shoes and plunge out into the freezing world again.

But you know, there's a warmth and comfort found in fellowship with God that you can wear, whether plodding through the snow or pushing a vacuum cleaner.

"It's a fellowship that grows warmer and more comfortable the longer we wear it. And the more time spent with God, the more comfortable we are in His presence. His Word warms our cold, aching hearts. His fellowship revives our humble spirits.

Communion with God never grows old and holey. It makes us grow **bold and holy**—and oh, so warm!

"The God of all comfort . . . comforts us in all our tribulation, that we may be able to comfort those who are in any trouble, by the comfort by which we ourselves are comforted of God" (2 Corinthians 1:3b,4).

22

SEEDS

"Boy, Mom, just wait till October," my little nature boy said one morning after watering his garden. "We'll have the biggest and best jack-o'-lantern in the whole wide world. Come out and see how the pumpkin vines are growing," he said, pulling at my hand.

He was quite a gardener. The vines were doing great, and there were yellow blossoms on some of them, the promise of coming fruit.

"Wasn't it lucky that I found some pumpkin seeds in the drawer, Mom?"

"You found them? I don't remember seeing any packages of pumpkin seeds."

"Well, they weren't in a package. They were just sittin' there."

"Are you sure they were pumpkin seeds?" I asked, trying to remember if I'd ever bought any.

"Sure, I eat 'em all the time, I know how they look," he said, drawing himself up to his full four feet.

We watched patiently as the "pumpkins" grew. They weren't round. They weren't orange. "They will be—just give 'em time," he said. But the longer we waited, the longer they grew. Did you ever see a zucchini jack-o'-lantern?

"But, Mom, I thought they were pumpkin seeds," said a disappointed gardener. "Why didn't I get a pumpkin?"

"Well, Honey, it's a law of nature—you get what

23

you plant, no matter how hard you were thinking 'pumpkin.' "

That night Daddy brought home the biggest pumpkin we ever saw. It wasn't quite the same as growing your own, but it was the biggest jack-o'-lantern in the whole wide world.

Yes, we reap what we sow. Have I planted the seeds of faith and obedience to God in the hearts of my children? Or will I someday reap the fruits of discontent and fear? Time will tell.

"Be not deceived; God is not mocked: for whatever a man sows, that shall he also reap (Galatians 6:7).

Today's Scripture: Luke 24:13-32

MONDAY

It started out as a typical "Three M" day—Monday Morning Mess. I knew I'd be busy most of the morning cleaning and washing, but I never dreamed I would be moving the refrigerator.

It began as we talked about the half-gallon jug of root beer I had bought the night before. We usually avoided soft drinks in favor of milk and water, but we had decided it would be fun to have a special treat. (Whoever heard of a "water float"?)

Christy was especially excited—so excited she couldn't wait till evening. A sneak preview was in order. She grasped the neck of the bottle with her small fingers (too small to reach around it) and lifted the jug from its place of honor on the top shelf of the refrigerator. As if not wanting to be choked, the bottle slipped from her fingers and crashed to the floor, with glass flying in every direction—and liquid spreading out in an undefinable pattern. It bubbled and sizzled its way under the refrigerator.

The next hour was spent in mopping, not only root beer from the floor, but also tears from big blue eyes that brimmed over with the loss of an expected treat.

Has anyone ever considered doing away with Mondays?

Some call it "Blue Monday," and some call it *Monday Morning Mess*, but I really think that as Christians, Monday ought to be one of our best days of the week. After all, if Sunday is spent worshiping God and feasting on His Word, we should be so filled up and fortified that not even a half-gallon of root beer on the kitchen floor will dampen our spirits!

We certainly don't plan on trouble, but we know it's inevitable—even on Friday and Saturday—and we can be ready to face it. Have you ever answered the question, "How are you today?" with the words, "Fine, under the circumstances." Well, that's no place to be! In Christ, we rise above the circumstances. We are in Him.

Sunday through Saturday, God's Word declares, "But God, who is rich in mercy, for His great love with which He loved us, even when we were dead in sins, has made us alive together with Christ (by grace you are saved) and has raised us up together, and made us sit together in heavenly places in Christ Jesus" (Ephesians 2:4-6).

So what if it's Monday—come on up!

A CRACKED CUP

Why had I put that cup in the back corner of the cupboard? I turned it over and over in my hands. It was so pretty—orange with white swirls. Many years ago, my little girl had bought it with money she'd saved. I was proud of it and her. Why had it been shoved to the back of the cupboard?

Then I remembered. It had a hairline crack, too small to see, but little droplets of liquid oozed out, leaving a ring on the table. I was afraid to use the cup anymore because the pressure of hot coffee might cause it to break. But I couldn't throw it away. It was a love-gift. So there it sat, loved but useless.

God often has to put us on the shelf, back in a dark corner, because a hairline crack, too small for others to see, has appeared. It's just a little crack, a little sin, but the life begins to seep out through it. That little sin, unconfessed, grows bigger each day until one day under the pressure of circumstances, we break.

Our loving heavenly Father sees our weakness, but doesn't disown us. We are eternally His, bought by His Son. And in His grace He places us on the shelf, useless but loved.

But there the likeness ends. My cup will *remain* useless, but God holds out hope for His child: "My grace is sufficient for you."

We must be willing to admit our sin and cast ourselves upon the grace and forgiveness of God. He will forgive and cleanse us, then reinstate us to a place of usefulness and service. His grace is the glue that keeps us from cracking up.

"My grace is sufficient for you, for my strength is made perfect in weakness." (2 Corinthians 12:9a).

Today's Scripture: Ephesians 1:5,6

MIRROR

"I hate to have my picture taken. It doesn't look a bit like me." Have you ever said that? Boy, I sure have. I just got some pictures back the other day, and the developing solution must have dripped, because there were funny lines between my eyebrows (surely not wrinkles). And the lighting must have been wrong, because one eye looked bigger than the other, and my hair looked dull and listless.

Is the image I have of myself a true one, or have I been closing my eyes to reality? I see what I want to see. I never frown or sulk at my mirror. I tilt my head back and put on my sweetest smile, and the lady smiling back at me looks a little like Farrah Fawcett. Why don't my pictures look like that?

Maybe it's time to take inventory. How am I coming across to others? Do they see me as the gentle, kind soul I'd like to be? Perhaps my opinionated self-centeredness is showing.

What does God see? I have to face up to it—I'm not a Farrah Fawcett, but I *am* a child of God. Looking into that mirror, I admit I'm no beauty queen, but I am God's temple, and as such I can be free from self-centered pride. So let them take pictures. It's the real me!

I know it's not always easy to accept ourselves as we are, especially if we don't like what we see. But not only can God help us to be content with our looks and status, but He will show us how to change those things that need changing.

"Mirror, mirror on the wall, who's the fairest one of all?" The answer: "Jesus, the fairest of ten thousand!" And I am in Him.

"Thou art fairer than the children of men: grace is poured into Thy lips; therefore God hath blessed Thee forever." (Psalm 45:2).

29

EGGS

"Separate four eggs and beat until stiff." I've always had trouble separating eggs, and when I read the recipe for meringue, I had second thoughts. Oh, well, live dangerously!

The first one was perfect. I nicked the yoke of the second egg, and a little yellow swirled into the bowl. The third, another success; but the fourth—well, so what if the meringue would be off-white?

The color wasn't the main problem, though: the white wouldn't whip up to stiff peaks. Was complete separation that important? (I ended up putting whipped cream on the pie!)

God says that separation for the Christian *is* important. "Come out from among them, and be separate." The teaching isn't popular today, and our lives show it. We don't stand firm and tall, and we have a slight tinge of yellow.

It *costs* something to be separate from the world. It costs some of the pleasures we've indulged in, some close friendships that pull us down, and some time and effort (usually spent on self-gratification) to learn God's will and walk in His way. It may even cost the understanding of loved ones and fellow Christians. God doesn't want us to be holier-than-thou, but He does command, "Be holy, for I am holy." And that's what separation is all about.

True, it's a separation *from* the world, but it's primarily a separation *unto* God. The enticements which the world dangles before our eyes pale in the presence of the Holy Son of God.

Christianity is not a list of "can't dos," for we have a *can-do* way of life ("I can do all things through Christ, who strengthens me"). If we love the Lord with all our heart, all our strength, and all our mind, we can do anything we want to.

Do you find your feet leading you into worldly pursuits and pleasures? Separate yourself to God. Love Him supremely and watch your desires change.

"Touch not the unclean thing, and I will receive you, and will be a Father to you, and you shall be my sons and daughters, says the Lord Almighty" (2 Corinthians 6:17b, 18).

Today's Scripture: John 3:1-7

THE NEW BABY

"Look!" my teenage son said, holding the baby's hand; "they look like real fingers!"

"They *are*, silly."

"Oh, Mom, her skin is so soft you can't even feel it!" my 12-year-old observed.

"Where's her teeth, Mommy?" asked my inquisitive kindergartner.

"They're still in her head," answered her wise eight-year-old sister. "Don't you know nothin'?"

31

The new baby's 10-year-old brother peeked around the corner. "Can I take it outside and show it to my friends?"

"Not today, honey," I sighed; "maybe later."

As the children temporarily lost interest and set out to pursue more exciting activities, I picked up my new baby and sank into the rocking chair, my tired body relaxing for the first time in several days.

Who was this soft bundle nestled against my shoulder? My lips brushed over the downy fuzz on her tiny head. I inhaled the sweet, pure fragrance of her newness. She was so helpless, so pliable.

Yes, she had real fingers and toes, real eyes and nose. She was a real person—a person to be loved and trained, a person with an eternal soul. What a blessing!

As I basked in the beauty of the moment alone with my new baby, I thought how God must feel toward the new babies in His family. How He loves His born-again ones, whatever their age or background! He nurtures them tenderly and patiently, hovering over them like a protective mother.

I remember those first days as a child in God's family. His presence was so real; His touch of love and restraint was so tender. But as I've grown stronger, He has allowed me to make decisions—and mistakes. When I fall, He picks me up, and when I stray, He leads me back to the narrow way. I'm His responsibility now, for He is my Father.

Is He yours? Have you been born into God's family? Come to Him today, simply as a child to his father. Through faith in the death, burial, and resurrection of Jesus Christ, you can know the love and guidance of God for today and always.

"The Spirit itself bears witness with our spirit, that we are the children of God" (Romans 8:16).

32

THE MUSIC BOX

"How dry I am; how dry I am." The tune tinkled from the corner of the room. Suddenly all eyes were on the pastor's wife, her face red with embarrassment and surprise. In her hands she held a beautiful ceramic beer stein, a birthday gift from her "secret pal."

The ladies gathered for a missionary meeting buzzed with, "Who could have given *that* to the pastor's wife?" and, "How funny! I wonder what pastor will say!"

Rusty cornered me. "Oh, I'm so embarrassed! I'm her secret pal—and I can't explain what happened."

"What *did* happen?" I asked, looking over her shoulder at the *thing* as it continued its merry tune.

"Well, I picked out a darling boy and girl on a teeter-totter for her music-box collection, and the clerk had to get one from the storage room. When she brought out the sealed box and asked if I wanted to check the contents, I said I was in a hurry and told her to wrap it up." Rusty blushed. "A beer stein! Well, I'm sure she doesn't have another one like it."

We're glad our pastor's wife has a sense of humor. She put us all at ease with her laugher. "What a great conversation piece when visiting missionaries come to dinner!"

I'm not sure that Rusty will want to reveal herself as the "unusual secret pal," but I'll bet she's learned one thing from this—examine the contents before buying the package!

We're exhorted to examine ourselves to see whether we are walking in the faith as revealed through Jesus Christ. Is He the Savior and Lord of our lives? Are we living in His will? We can thoroughly examine ourselves in the light of the Word of God—and buy the whole package.

"Examine yourselves, whether you are in the faith; prove your own selves" (2 Corinthians 13:5).

Today's Scripture: James 3:1-10

FIRE

Sparks, like tiny ballerinas, pirouetted above the flames and danced up the chimney, soon to burn out and disappear. I gazed at the burning log in the fireplace as its warmth spread over my body and through the room. I loved to watch.

A fire under control is beautiful and beneficial, but when out of hand it can bring disaster and death. James likened the human tongue to a fire. I can see why. We have the power to warm and soothe hearts or to burn and destroy human spirits—just by our tongues.

As a Christian, I must keep my tongue under control. No longer can I speak my mind when I feel like it. Those harsh words, like sparks igniting a flame, should be controlled. Why? What difference does it make?

Now I am an ambassador of Jesus Christ. The words, the sounds, that come from my mouth are representative of the King of Glory (or the Prince of darkness).

I think we could cut down on air pollution if more of us kept our mouths shut. It's so simple to be verbose. I did it again yesterday. I expressed my opinion, without invitation, to my married daughter. She, lovely Christian that she is, was quiet, and let me ramble on as I attacked her ideas. It was easier to spill my thoughts at that moment than it was later in the day when I called her to apologize.

Although she graciously forgave me for speaking out of turn, the words have no doubt done their harm. She may be more careful in the future about sharing her plans with me. She will probably be on guard so she won't get burned (by my tongue) again. I know. I've had the same thing happen to me.

Let's bring that tongue under the control of the Holy Spirit today. He's the only One strong enough to tame such an unruly member.

"Let the words of my mouth and the meditation of my heart be acceptable in Thy sight, O Lord, my strength and my Redeemer" (Psalm 19:14).

TELEPHONE

"Yeah, Gert, I'm on the prayer chain. Sure, I have time to listen. Who has a request for prayer? Bob's leaving Mary? You're kidding! How come? Another woman? How's she taking it? I thought there was something wrong there. Did I tell you about the time I saw. . . .?"

Yes, I would pray for both of them. They could count on me. As I hung up, I thought what a good thing it was that we had started a prayer chain in our church. How else can you know what's going on, and whom to pray for? A few people got upset when they heard we were discussing their problems . . . but they must be unspiritual.

"Oh, hello, Gert. I just thought of a prayer request too. You know our pastor is thinking about buying a new car. He really should get a second-hand one, so let's pray. . . ."

We called them prayer requests, but we knew it was really gossip, plain, and simple. What a trap to fall into! And what excruciating withdrawal pains to abstain from idle talk. My jaws grind and twitch as I clench my teeth, trying to keep bad news to myself.

I'm not saying we shouldn't pray. And neither am I condemning prayer chains, rightfully used. We do need each other's concerned prayers, but we don't need our weaknesses aired via the telephone lines.

I used to think that talebearing was solely a feminine trait, but it just isn't so, no matter how much men may deny their participation in gossip prayer requests. We can all be delivered from this common problem by taking our news to the Lord. There in His presence our motives will be purified, and we can learn to pray in love rather than prattle in lust.

Yes, it is lust to talk about others—lust for attention, for power, and for a sense of superiority that we haven't succumbed to the same frailties as our brothers and sisters.

Let's not be talebearers, but burden-bearers.

"Bear one another's burdens, and so fulfill the law of Christ" (Galatians 6:2).

CRAYONS

When Kathy was two years old, I bought her first box of crayons. She was so pleased as she took each one out, carefully inspected it, and gently fit it back into the box.

"See, Honey," I said, pointing to one color at a time, "this is red, and this is blue."

"I like this one," she lisped; "what's this?"

"That's yellow."

"Oh—lallo. I like lallo!"

Later, when I looked at her masterpieces, I found that she had colored every page of her new coloring book with blobs of yellow! She was so proud of her artistry.

She eventually learned to keep the color within the lines, but she only used—you guessed it—lallo. There were yellow apples, balls, and cups. There were yellow dogs, elephants, and flowers. Kathy liked "lallo."

I don't know if yellow is still her favorite color, but as she matured, she gained such an appreciation for color and design that she became an art teacher.

As Christians, we need to mature too—in our knowledge and love of God, in our prayers (still self-centered?), and in our service (afraid to try something new for God?).

We can be bold in Christ, stepping out in faith, trying new things—new studies, new friends, new ministries, and even new songs. We can grow up in Christ without growing old.

38

God's Spirit is always new and fresh, and as we allow Him to control our lives today, *now*, we will discover an adventure in living that we never dreamed possible. Let's enjoy the full range of God's spectrum today! It will take courage and determination to step out, but our God is always with us, and He will give us grace to obey His leading.

". . . Be no longer children, tossed to and fro and carried about with every wind of doctrine . . . but, speaking the truth in love . . . grow up into Him in all things, who is the Head, even Christ" (Ephesians 4:14,15).

Today's Scripture: Deuteronomy 32:11,12)

KITTY

I must be getting lazy. My idea of a good time is relaxing in my favorite chair with my feet up, and stroking my furry-purry cat.

We're both pretty independent all day, greeting each other with an occasional pat or rub, and of course our paths cross at mealtimes. But our special rendezvous is after the dinner dishes are done and I stretch out to read.

My feet on the hassock is her signal to jump up on my lap. And she acts like she owns me! She turns this way and that at least twice—poking and pushing until she finds just the right spot. Then she flops down and stretches her long, heavy body the length of my legs. Balanced precariously, with her head almost to my feet, she holds on tightly to keep from slipping off. Then her motor starts, vibrating her contentment. I'm content, too—for about a half an hour.

Since our calico is an indoor cat, she doesn't get much exercise and weighs a solid 14 pounds. "Oh, Kitty, you're too heavy. My legs are breaking," I groan, shifting my position. "That's enough for today—there's always tomorrow." A dirty look over her shoulder, one last squeeze with her claws, and down she thumps onto the floor.

Like Kitty, we too have familiar rituals that we cherish. Good health, good weather, good times. But God may sometimes shift us around, changing our lifestyles—not because He's uncomfortable, but because He knows what's best for us.

Even if things aren't going our way, we don't have to get our claws out. Instead, we can trust God's wisdom for today, and look for a brighter tomorrow.

"Be of good courage, and He shall strengthen your heart, all you that hope in the Lord" (Psalm 31:24).

LOCKS

A crime took place in our neighborhood recently—a heinous crime. The criminal got away and still hasn't been found. He has committed this same atrocity over 20 times in a nearby city, and the police are baffled.

"How does he get away? Where will he strike next?" The people are fearful. "Why don't they catch him? Will our homes be invaded by this dark evil? What should we do to protect ourselves?"

There was an immediate run on locks. The locksmiths couldn't keep up with the orders. We put extra locks on our doors too: deadbolts; pins through the sliding-glass doors; chains and latches. When the locks sold out, people began to buy dogs—big, loud dogs. Some were even driven to purchase guns.

Fear is a numbing and enervating passion that has brought many repercussions. Children have been locked out of their own homes. Women have shot at noises in the dark. And neighbors have been attacked by dogs. This is the age we live in. Men's hearts fail them for fear. The world has gone crazy. What can we do?

Jesus said, "Look up, for your redemption draws near." It is our obligation to protect ourselves and our families; to do otherwise would be foolish. But we don't need to be *controlled* by fear. Our safety does not rest in locks and watchdogs; our confidence is in the Lord God Almighty. He will deliver us from the snare of the fowler, and from the noisome pestilence

41

(Psalm 91:3). Our loving heavenly Father holds us in the hollow of His hand.

Does this mean that, as Christians, we are immune to heartache and suffering? No. But it does mean that we do not need to fear. God is with us in all our tribulations.

Jesus died at the hands of vicious criminals—death on the cross. God did not rescue Him from suffering and anguish, but He did deliver Him from the bonds of death. He lives today.

You and I, though our lives take unwelcome paths of trouble, may confidently put our trust in Him, and not be afraid. If fear does invade our hearts, we may say,

"When I am afraid, I will trust in Thee" (Psalm 56:3).

Today's Scripture: Romans 14:1-10

ELECTRIC BLANKET

Wind howled around the corners of the house. Rain pelted the windows. I had always wanted an electric blanket, and tonight was the night to try it out for the first time. It was a super-deluxe model with dual controls. I had adjusted the temperature about half an hour before bedtime so we could get the benefits right away. My husband likes to sleep a little cooler than I, so he snuggled down into his side with the number 3 heat setting, and I settled down wiht my number 5 setting.

I don't know how long we'd been asleep when I awoke cold and shivering. My hair felt like it was standing on end. I reached over and moved the dial to number 7. But the longer I waited the colder I got.

My husband tossed and turned and threw off the blankets, while I wrapped myself up into a tighter ball.

"Honey," he finally gasped. "I'm suffocating! This thing's burning me up—and I have it turned to 'OFF'.

Something's definitely wrong. I'm freezing to death, and I have mine turned up to number 10!"

"Do you suppose . . .?" He began to laugh, then jumped up to turn on the light. "Yes, that's it! You've got the controls mixed up. We've been adjusting the wrong dials!"

I laughed, "And here I've been judging you as hot-headed."

"And I thought you were cold-blooded."

That wasn't the only time I've wrongly judged my husband, or vice versa. I used to think he wasn't as "spiritual" as I because he didn't react the same way to God's voice. He thought I was too emotional because my tears come easily. I thought his prayers were too quick and to the point; he thought mine were too drawn-out and wordy.

After several years of misunderstanding, we realized that we operate on different wavelengths. Not only do we respond differently because of our sex, but also because of our personalities and upbringing.

Now that we accept the fact of our differences, we are adjusting our thermostats. The problem of judging one another according to our own personal standards is solved (almost).

This attitude can extend to our children, our neighbors, our friends, and even to those whose form of worship may be different from ours. Too emotional? Too cold? Not necessarily. We just have different thermostats.

"Judge not, that you be not judged" (Matthew 7:1).

Today's Scripture: John 3:18-21

COBWEBS

"Boy, your mother really made it look scary in here," I heard a little girl say from the living room. I hadn't decorated in there. What did she mean?

"Mom, where did you get such a real-looking spider web?" my daughter asked, pointing to the lamp. "It looks so spooky!"

Spooky? My eyes followed her finger to a gray, wispy mass. She was right. A real-life Halloween spider web was draped from ceiling to lampshade. But I hadn't put it there; it had been there all along, and it showed up by turning on the not-often-used lamp on the stereo.

"Oh, look, Barby," the little darling said, turning her attention to me; "your mom has such rosy cheeks. Are you going to be a clown for Halloween, Mrs. Cook?"

"No, Schweetie," I hissed, dropping a piece of bubble gum in her bag and gently escorting her to the door. "Come back again—next year!"

And honesty is supposed to such an adorable trait in children! My housekeeping (abilities?) had come to light. The cobweb had been growing without my knowledge, and not until the light was turned on was it (and I) found out. Maybe I'd better turn on some more lights and get out my duster!

The light of God's Word shows me the sin that's crept into my life, and if I hide from that light, it will thrive and grow in my darkened corners. So I'd better turn to God's Word daily, reading and prayerfully meditating upon its truths. By keeping my life clean, I won't embarrass myself—or my heavenly Father.

"But he who does truth comes to the light, so that his deeds may be made shown that they are done in God" (John 3:21).

Today's Scripture: Lamentations 3:22-26

KNICK-KNACKS

Rabbits, rabbits, rabbits—porcelain, pewter, and

paper mache! My collection of the past few years stands, lies, and crouches on glass shelves in the corner curio cabinet. *Hmm, they've certainly multiplied!* There are other knick-knacks displayed, too: several china cups and saucers, an old silver tea set, and an antique vase. My curios are also spread throughout the house, and although they represent very little monetarily, to me they're precious because most of them are love gifts.

There's a little blue handmade pillow that Becky designed in eighth grade, and a carved gazelle from Barby's trip with a neighbor friend. And I could never part with the red tray Danny created in machine shop or the breadboard Greg made when he was 12. Then there's the pot Kathy threw on the potter's wheel, and the greeting cards Christy has composed over the years, and the ginger jar Les gave me, and the. . . .

We all save things—perhaps too many things—that we've picked up in souvenir shops or along the seashore. Most of them wouldn't bring bottom dollar in a garage sale, but to us they're special because of the memories they evoke, the sentimental value we attach to them.

I wonder if we've stored up God's treasures in the same way: a special verse, a song, a blessing—closed away in a curio cabinet to be admired. We don't use them; we just save them. Perhaps on special occasions we show them off, but then we return them to their place on the shelf.

But how about today? Who is God to me today? Did I seek His face? Have I a fresh word from His Book? What neighbor am I praying for *now*? Memories as well as souvenirs are reminders of days gone by, and we cherish them, but as children of the *living* God,

47

we need to remember that He is always present. We must believe that he *is*, and not just that He *was*.

Today let's throw open the doors of our curio cabinets and allow the fresh, cool breeze of the Holy Spirit to blow the dust off our stagnant "knick-knack" experiences and fill us with a new awareness of Him—an awareness to take the dusty things off the shelf and share them with others.

"O sing unto the Lord a new song, for He has done marvelous things; His right hand and His holy arm have gotten Him the victory" (Psalm 98:1).

Today's Scripture: 2 Corinthians 12:6-10

SANDPAPER

"Swish, swish. Swoosh, swoosh." My husband bent over the pine gate-leg table, intent on his sanding job. He had almost finished his latest project.

"You think this'll make a good wedding present for the kids, Honey?" he asked, looking up from his work, his hair and eyebrows white with sawdust.

"It's beautiful!" I said, gliding my hand across the smooth finish. "But aren't you through sanding?"

"No, not yet. I can still feel a couple of rough spots."

I flipped through his stack of sandpapers. Some had

large grains of sand, "for extremely rough surfaces," he said. The one he had been using was almost velvety.

"This one doesn't have any grain on it; how can it do any good?"

"It's for the finishing touch. That last little bit of smoothing—anything rougher would ruin it."

God knows just the right kind of pressure I need in my life too, like a fine cabinetmaker.

> There is so much in me
> That needs to be made smooth;
> My dear Lord works patiently
> The rough spots to remove.
>
> He sends the ones I love
> To say the things that grieve;
> I may resist their words
> Or as His will—receive.
>
> If I can just remember
> 'Tis my Lord who's trying me,
> Not to destroy my will
> But to shape it tenderly.
>
> Lord, I yield to each rebuke
> And praise Thy holy Name
> For using Thy sandpaper
> That our wills may be the same.

"Every valley shall be exalted, and every mountain and hill shall be made low; and the crooked shall be made straight, and the rough places plain" (Isaiah 40:4).

Today's Scripture: 2 Corinthians 3:14-18

FOG

I looked out my kitchen window. Draped over the trees and drifting across the lawn, the fog hung like a gossamer veil. Whispering breezes ruffled the gray dampness, revealing a glimpse of the house across the street. The fog is quietly beautiful to me safe inside my home, but to those who must travel the freeways, it can be deadly.

Several months of the year, this veil nestles down in our valley, hiding the sun and overworking the Highway Patrol as they direct traffic through the cotton-like shroud. What a relief when the fog lifts and the bright sunshine, that was there all along, beams its warm rays over our city!

Sometimes we take a trip to the mountains, braving the fog until we get above it. What a joy to find the sun shining there! Down below, our valley looks like a big bowl of cream-of-wheat, and we dread the return trip home.

For many years I lived in a fog, the veil of self-will hiding the Son of God from me. Then one day the Holy Spirit showed me that the veil had been ripped—the Bible says "from top to bottom"—revealing Christ, the God-Man who died for my sins.

I don't *have* to live in darkness anymore, but I sometimes turn from Him and stumble into the valley of deadly fog. How foolish to think I could ever find satisfaction in those damp surroundings when once I've seen and lived in God's light!

50

As Christians we can push aside that veil of the self-life and enter into God's presence. Let's live there today, loving and praising Him, and drawing back the veil for others who are still groping around in the fog.

"And behold, the veil of the temple was torn in two from top to bottom; and the earth quaked and the rocks split" (Matthew 27:51).

Today's Scripture: Titus 3:4-7

WHITE SHOES

"Do I look all right, Mom? I feel so important in these white shoes."

I studied my teenage daughter as she preened before me, ready to leave for her first job. It wasn't exactly what she had hoped for (it was a job in a serve-yourself restaurant), but she had gotten it by herself. And I was pleased as she stood straight and tall in her white shoes and uniform.

"I'll get a red apron to wear too," she said, tugging at her nylons and brushing off the white shoes again.

It's a happy time, that first job. It was a little scary, not only for her, but for me too. She was no longer entirely dependent on me and my wallet. Oh, it's been a long time since I've had to brush her hair and tie her shoes, but at least she needed me to supply her allowance, and those little extras, like money for football games and pizza after church. But now. . . .

We all have to grow up. It doesn't mean that she no longer needs or loves me, but that she's been growing and planning toward this day when she could stand on her own feet. Although she will continually grow more independent of me, she will always need to depend on God and so will I. We never outgrow our need for Him.

There have been times (too many) when I thought I could handle a situation by myself. I didn't need God. But I often tripped and fell on my face. And today, though I am maturing, it's not *apart from* Him, but *in* Him, growing more like Jesus day by day as I trust in His indwelling presence.

"Let him who thinks he stands take heed lest he fall" (1 Corinthians 10:12).

COOKIES

"Wait till you hear what I did to my brother!" a neighbor girl squealed.

I knew I shouldn't eavesdrop, but I was curious.

"You know he eats everything I bake before anyone else gets a chance to taste it. What a pig! Anyway, I got him this time."

"What? What did you do?" asked my daughter.

"Well," her voice dropped, "I baked some chocolate chip cookies last night and. . . ." Laughter. "And in place of the chocolate chips I put little chunks of Ex-Lax!"

"You're kidding!"

"No. And of course he ate most of them before he went to bed. Funny, he says he has the stomach flu today!"

Well, I can't say I approve of her solution to her brother's gluttony, but it proves one thing—you can't believe everything you see.

There are many religions that look good today. They offer peace of mind, success, and freedom. They talk about God, life, and fulfillment. Yet their candy-coated lies have disastrous results—deadly results.

Followers may find self-realization, but not God-realization. Perhaps the disciples of false religions even seem holier, kinder, and more blessed than genuine Christians. But the proof is in the eating.

To swallow the claims of any group not founded on the Word of God *alone* is to ask for trouble—not just temporary trouble that will pass away like "stomach flu," but eternal trouble that has no antidote or cure.

Don't make the mistake of believing everything you see, hear, or taste. Test it with the Word of God. What do they teach about Jesus Christ? Who is He? What is the way to heaven? What about sin?

"Thy Word was unto me the joy and rejoicing of my heart, for I am called by Thy Name, O Lord God of hosts" (Jeremiah 15:16).

Today's Scripture: Exodus 3:13-15

A CUP OF COFFEE

Every now and then I think about giving up coffee. I know it's not nutritious, and it's gotten so expensive. Who needs it anyway? I'm not an addict: two cups in the morning, sometimes one in the afternoon, and two more in the evening. *Surely that's not enough to hurt anyone,* I argue with myself.

Why do I keep drinking it when I have these doubts? Well, there's more to a cup of coffee than caffeine and high prices.

It's not just the same thing to visit with an old friend over a glass of water. And warming chilled hands around a hot cup of coffee in those wee gray hours of a winter's morning warms the heart as well.

Some of my favorite times with my husband have been over a late-night cup of coffee with the children tucked securely in their beds. Our tense nerves and bodies relax as we share our hopes and worries while sipping at the warm drink.

The pot's always on at our house, ready to welcome unexpected guests or to offer an excuse to sit down and plan what to do after the wash is folded and put away.

I'm sure we won't drink coffee together when we're in heaven, but we will have that sweet fellowship and warmth that today's friendships foreshadow.

In that day, just a look at the Savior will warm our spirits. There'll be no need for a cup of hot coffee to melt away tensions, for the Lord Himself will be all we ever need or long for.

Do you long for fellowship today? God said, "I AM." Are you tired? Do you feel like giving up? "I AM." Do you ache for understanding? "I AM."

A cup of coffee may be a pleasure that you enjoy, but only a personal relationship with the God of heaven can bring lasting contentment and answers to the problems of life.

Why don't you drop in and we'll talk about it — over a cup of coffee?

"God said to Moses. . . .Thus you shall say to the children of Israel: I AM has sent me to you' " (Exodus 3:14).

SUNGLASSES

"Where could I have put them?" I mumbled, rummaging first through my purse, then the junk drawer. "I wore them yesterday afternoon. Maybe I left them in the car."

"Mom, come here, quick! —Please hurry!" Excited voices called to me from the down the hall. What could be the matter? Had one of the girls hurt herself? As I reached Becky's room, she slowly opened the door. "Mom, look. Did you ever see anything so funny?"

There were my sunglasses—on the cat. She sat, sphinx-like, in the center of the bed, a red bandana tied under her chin, peering suspiciously through my dark glasses. Not a hair quivered. Not an eye winked. She was the Cinderella of the cat-set. This was her moment.

As we broke into peals of laughter, Kitty came to life and pounced off the bed, leaving her scarf and glasses for some young prince to find. Once again she was just a cat sitting by the hearth.

There are times when we all feel special, like Cinderella. In those moments we rise above our usual capabilities and shine as God intended us to.

Whether we choose sunglasses or a new outfit to give us that extra pizzazz, it seems worth the effort, although inside we know it's only a temporary euphoria.

When the clock strikes midnight, we flee back into

our old familiar ruts, satisfied with rags and trivialities.

I think God has more for His children than a fairy-tale fabrication. He says to get rid of the old way of life and "put on the new man, which after God is created in righteousness and true holiness" (Ephesians 4:24). And we're to *leave* it on. There's no need to grovel again, no need to look for artificial trappings to build our self-confidence.

Our confidence is in the Lord. We can always be our best, clothed not in sunglasses and bandana, but in the righteousness of God.

"Put on the Lord Jesus Christ, and make no provision for the flesh, to fulfill its lusts" (Romans 13:14).

Today's Scripture: Psalm 139:1-6

PORTRAIT

"Greg, leave him alone. Danny, stop teasing the baby." Oh, dear, Baby is slobbering on her new dress. "Kathy, don't tease your sister. Becky and Christy, look at the camera."

Snap, goes the shutter. Les and I, trying to keep the children in control, lost control of ourselves.

What a hassle! We so much wanted to give our friends a picture that really looked like us. Or did we? We wanted a picture of us at our best—all of us with pleasant smiles.

Although our picture-taking project turned out to be a catastrophe (not only for us but also for the photographer), I think I learned something—something more important than a posed picture of our family not being ourselves.

God loves us just as we are. No matter what kind of a pretty face we try to present to others, He knows us —and still loves us. Each one. Individually.

Of course we want to present a pleasing picture to others, but God knows our every weakness. It gives me such a sense of freedom to know that He not only knows and loves me, but that He can do something about my weaknesses and failures. And not only mine, but my family's as well.

Each person is even more precious to Him than to me. I admit I worry about my children. I worry about the kinds of adults they'll be and the kinds of lives they'll live. But God doesn't worry. He knows, and He cares.

He knows us, and He wants us to know Him. And we *can* know Him through His Word, the Bible—a portrait of God.

It's true that neither my children nor their parents are perfect pictures of the perfect family, but God knows this and is working in our lives. Let Him work in yours today! He knows you inside and out—and still He loves you.

"Search me, O God, and know my heart: try me, and know my thoughts" (Psalm 139:23).

58

QUIETNESS

It's early morning. The rest of the family is still snuggled down in their beds. I sit in the living room, alone and quiet. As a mother of a large family, I've learned that the only way to be alone is to rise extra early or go to bed extra late. I enjoy both, but have a problem with the second choice—I fall asleep before I have a chance to enjoy my solitude!

I like to listen to the early-morning sounds, before the roar of lawn mowers and freeway traffic fills the air. On early summer mornings I hear the call of a mother robin, her low chirp reminding her babies to be patient. She's on her way with a medium-rare worm or an over-easy grub. The babies return her call with high-pitched tweets.

How great is our God! Even these busy birds are precious in His sight. "Are not two sparrows (robins, too?) sold for a farthing? And one of them shall not fall on the ground without your Father."

There are other sounds, too. Two dogs bark their early morning woofs. Maybe they're planning a rendezvous if one of them can escape his confinement when the meter-reader comes through the backyard gate!

There aren't many outside sounds this time of day, and I concentrate on listening to those sounds around the house—sounds that are so ordinary, so familiar, that I hardly hear them. There is the hum of the refrigerator, the soft padding of cat paws across the rug, the clock ticking away.

Time is passing. The sun is rising higher in the sky. Other household sounds interrupt my reverie. A closet door clicks shut. The water, hot and cold, rushes through the pipes, merges together, then sprays a warm refreshment over my husband.

I yawn and stretch. Time to fix breakfast. Time to lay aside my solitude and begin my service. I pray that I'll be more ready to meet the requirements of the day because of my few minutes of quietness.

The tempo of living this day has been set by a chirp, a bark, a hum, a soft step, and a ticking. My ears are sharp and ready to hear a silent cry for help, an unspoken word of love, a guiding Voice.

God gave us *two* ears for listening and *one* mouth for talking. Do you suppose there's a lesson in that?

"Be still and know that I am God . . ." (Psalm 46:10a).

Today's Scripture: 1 Corinthians 12:14-18

POTATOES

"I can't look a potato straight in the eye anymore," Donna whispered as she passed the bowl of mashed potatoes back to me. "Jim and I didn't have much

money when we were first married, so I filled us up with potatoes." She smiled (or was that nausea?). "We had potatoes scalloped, whipped, creamed, and fried—every day. They were filling, all right," she added, patting her hips, "in more ways than one!"

Many young-marrieds find themselves in the same predicament. I fixed tuna casserole twice a week. Ramona served macaroni and cheese every night so she could splurge with a batch of fudge on Saturdays. As newlyweds, we had tried to prepare inexpensive meals, but had neglected the importance of nutrition and variety—and our husbands rebelled!

When we dared to be different, we ate better and had happier homes.

As Christians we can dare to be different too—different from the world and, yes, even different from each other.

God loves diversity. Consider the snowflake, the blades of grass, and the fingerprints of the billions of earth's inhabitants. Yet we often try to conform to other Christians in our likes and dislikes, even going so far as to emulate certain gifts of the Spirit. It's hard to imitate others, and it's as unappetizing as a constant diet of potatoes.

We can be ourselves, fully and wholly, in Christ. We're not all prayer warriors or Sunday school teachers. We're not all bubbly and vivacious or quiet and sober-minded. But we are all uniquely loved of God. When controlled by Him, our personalities and individuality can feed a hungry world—a world hungry for the fulfillment found in a Spirit-freed life.

"Now you are the body of Christ, and members in particular" (1 Corinthians 12:27).

WINDOWS

I'm glad for windows; they bring the outside in. I can sit in my living room and, without changing a thing, have a new decor four times a year. From December until about March, the muted tones of winter decorate one side of the room. Through the sliding glass door I see wisps of fog hanging in the long, spindly branches of the silver-leaf maple. Sparrows sit in a row, puffy and ball-like, on twigs. Occasionally they swoop down as a group to peck at the dry brown grass, hoping to find some seeds or breadcrumbs. Rain washes away the fog and drips down the window pane, clearing it for the soon-to-come hues of green.

Here and there tiny blades poke through the soft brown earth. In a few short months, red tulips, like bells, will wave in the warm spring breezes. More birds will visit our backyard, poking and pulling at long grasses with which to build their nests. I see life in my own backyard!

Then tulips are replaced by petunias and marigolds. Roses bloom profusely. All the colors of the rainbow flood my home. Fresh air blows in through the open window, and I feel a fresh new surge of life urging me on to new conquests.

The mornings become cool and crisp. Leaves turn various shades of gold and brown. One tree sports a brilliant, wine-colored foliage. I think I like autumn best of all. I feel so mellow. There are no lawns to mow, no gardens to weed, no trees to spray. Yet there's one job that gets me outside—leaves, leaves, and more leaves!

The seasons have completed their course. A small daisy hangs on, unwilling to face winter. But its time will come.

Time passes for all of us. We live, we learn, we grow, we plan, we love, we die. But how we use the days and the years God entrusts to us is all-important. We can see the beauty and the color of life through the windows of our souls and be enriched for all eternity, or we can close the drapes of our spirits and live in our own small, man-made world.

I want God to decorate my life as I pass from spring to winter. How about you?

"The winter is past; the rain is over and gone; the flowers appear on the earth; the time of the singing of birds is come, and the voice of the turtledove is heard in our land" (Song of Solomon 2:11,12).

Today's Scripture: Psalm 17:1-7

SHELVES

The other day while cleaning my youngest daughter's closet to get rid of her outgrown clothes, I came upon her secret shelf. There in neatly labeled boxes were "Christmas presents," "Diaries," "Letters," and "My favorite things."

I have to be honest—I was tempted for a minute to look. But then I remembered that many years ago I too had a secret shelf. On it I kept love letters, my diary, a bank full of quarters, and a few mementos from old boyfriends. My mother had respected my right to privacy, and I owed the same respect to my 11-year-old daughter.

We all need a special place to call our own, a place that other eyes never see, except maybe that one special friend who knows all our secrets anyway.

I have a secret shelf in my heart, too. Do you? It's a place where I keep my very special dreams and hurts. Sometimes I'm tempted to pull them off the shelf and parade them around to friends and family, but I know that though they are precious to me, to others they may look like worthless trinkets.

There is one special Friend who never laughs at the things on my secret shelf. As I show each one to Jesus, He sees the value they hold to me. He has shown me that some are worthless and need to be cleaned out to make room for those things that *do* deserve a place:

I'm glad for house cleaning days, when I can get into my closet and examine the corners of my secret shelf. And I'm glad my Lord never forces me to show Him what I'm saving there. He waits patiently for me to share my secrets with Him when I'm ready to. As I do, I see Him take my little mementos and change them into precious treasures.

This is my prayer for you, too—that you will share

your innermost thoughts and desires with the Lord of Glory. He is your best Friend, and He cares deeply about you—and all you have hidden on your secret shelf.

"Shall not God search this out? For He knows the secrets of the heart" (Psalm 44:21).

Today's Scripture: 2 Thessalonians 3:7-13

FURNACE

"I'll be careful, Daddy—honest," I called up the stairs as I ran to the furnace room.

"Well, stay back, then. That coal flying through the window could hurt you."

Coal day. I remember how I loved to watch the deliveryman roll it down the chute through our basement window. Hard. Black. Shiny. My fourth-grade teacher had described how long it took coal to form in the earth, and how hard it was for the miners to get it out. It always amazed me that it could burn, and I loved watching my dad shovel it into the furnace.

How easy we have it today in our modern homes! A

slight touch of the thermostat, and on goes the fire, heating the house thoroughly before we have a chance to wonder if it's cold out today.

It's easier to be spiritually fired up now, too. Our ancestors had to travel far over rough roads to church. Some of them had to wait for the itinerant preacher to come by before they could hear the Word of God. And that wasn't many years ago, either.

What progress has been made! Or has it! Do we really appreciate our churches? Do we value the Christian radio and TV programs that come into our homes at the flick of a switch? Those Christians-before-us paid a great price for our privileges, and we often take them for granted.

Today, in many parts of the world, men and women sacrifice great things (often their lives) for an opportunity to share the gospel. How far would I be willing to go for the Word of God? What price am I willing to pay? A few minutes before breakfast? An hour or two on Sunday?

What value do I place on God's Word? Do I take the time and effort to "shovel" it in, or am I still a bystander, idly watching as I did on coal day so many years go?

"Rise up, you women that are at ease; hear my voice, you careless daughters; listen to my speech" (Isaiah 32:9).

BULLETIN BOARD

I pinned the slip of paper on my bulletin board and stepped back for a better look. It was almost covered with letters and notes from publishing houses all over the country. Unfortunately, most of them were rejection slips.

I had put the bulletin board over my desk when I began writing for publication. At first there were writer's helps, article ideas, and several possible markets. But as I sent out my work and received it back again—and again—I began a collage of rejections. I had slips from *Saturday Evening Post* and *Reader's Digest,* as well as from small, unknown denominational magazines. It seemed that no one wanted my work, and my enthusiasm began to wane. Self-confidence was hidden by those rejection slips. That's when I made a decision.

From now on there would be no negative reminders on my bulletin board; only letters of encouragement and check stubs for published manuscripts would decorate that eye-level display.

Oh, there weren't many items hanging from brightly colored pins, but those few added to my confidence and self-esteem, until once more I wrote with encouragement and ease. I've learned that negative thoughts produce negative responses, and positive thoughts produce positive responses.

This truth carries over into other areas of life, too. When I think of how often I've failed at dieting, I've lost the battle before breakfast. Sad, defeating thoughts seem to attract trouble and gloom. My family also reflects my attitudes. An encouraging word for a hard-earned "C"; gives needed confidence that a "B" is possible. A cheerful kiss for my husband returning from work does a lot more for our evening than a word-of-complaint greeting.

Today is a good day to begin practicing positive thinking. It takes a definite act of the will because old, negative thought-patterns are hard to break.

The Apostle Paul gives us some principles in Philippians 4:8: "Whatever things are true, whatever things are honest, whatever things are just, whatever things are pure, whatever things are lovely, whatever things are of good report—if there is any virtue, and if there is any praise, think on these things."

Today's Scripture: Deuteronomy 6:6,7

BREAKFAST

I felt my way down the cold, dark hallway, turned on the kitchen light, blinked back the glare, and wondered why morning starts so early.

The coffee began to perk, its mellow fragrance filling the air. I watched the frying bacon suddenly come to life, bending, twisting, and crawling toward the center of the pan. It hissed and spewed little particles of grease as it reached a golden-brown perfection. I tenderly removed it from the pan and placed the strips alongside two eggs, sunny-side-up, staring blankly back at me. Each plate received its offering for the morning and lined up on both sides of the table, awaiting my family, the thundering herd.

Then they came, a myriad of colors and sounds—crunching, munching, slicing, and slurping. Just as quickly, they moved together as a mass, snatched the waiting brown bags from the counter, and made their exits, each going their separate ways.

There I sat in a stunned, yet glorious, silence, broken only by the dripping of the faucet, which my oldest son managed to accomplish every time he was near the sink. I wondered what I'd do after scraping the peanut butter off the breadboard and wiping up the eternally spilled milk from under the table. I was sure I'd think of something.

In the rush of beginning a new day, I wondered if I remembered to tell the children that I loved them—and that Jesus loves them. I wished I'd started earlier so we could have family devotions before meeting the world head-on. I sat at the table, visualizing each one, and I committed them to the Lord for His care. They are His, and no matter what comes into their lives, He is in control.

This happened several years ago, and most of the children are gone now. The breakfast table is almost empty. I wonder if they remember that I love them—

and that Jesus loves them. They are still His, and their lives are under His loving control.

Yes, morning does start early, but it's never too early to breakfast upon the Word of God—and share it with our children.

"Early will I seek Thee" (Psalm 63:1b).

Today's Scripture: Matthew 13:11-17

STEREO

I knew my husband was in the living room; I could hear the paper rattling. Why didn't he answer me?

"Honey, did you hear me? I'm going to bed now," I called. Silence.

I peered around the corner. There he sat, tapping his foot and whistling slightly off-tune. As I leaned in further, I could see why he didn't answer.

71

Like an astronaut awaiting instructions from Houston, his ears were covered with big black cups wired to the stereo.

I moved in front of him and mouthed, "Good night. I'm going to bed now."

Eyes widening, he jumped up to kiss me good night and caught my nostril on the edge of his headphone.

"Oh, I'm sorry, Honey," he exclaimed, pulling the apparatus off his head. "but just listen to this. It's beautiful."

I felt like I was in another world as the stereo music flowed into each ear. There were bells in the left ear and violins in the right—a combination that made me forget my sore nose.

How often do I open my ears to the music that daily surrounds me? I don't think to put on my spiritual earphones and really listen—listen to the birds chirping outside my window, or listen to the unspoken plea for understanding from a troubled friend.

Do I hear the leaves rustling against each other as a puff of wind passes through? Are my ears tuned to that still, small voice of God as He says, "This is the way; walk in it"?

A symphony of praise rings out today. The high notes reach up to heaven, and the loud, ominous strains touch the lives of men and women. All these sounds, joyful and sad, blend together as one, filling the spiritually tuned ears and hearts of all who will listen.

"Speak, for Thy servant hears" (1 Samuel 3:10b)

TINY SPIDER

"Help! Oh, Mom, come here—quick!"

At the sound of Becky's cry, my heart did an extra flump and my knees turned to water. Was there a Peeping Tom? Had she slammed her finger in the closet door? Had the letter she received this afternoon been bad news?

"What? What is it?" I exclaimed.

"Look!" she said, pointing toward the corner of the ceiling; "a spider!"

There it was, a spider no bigger than my thumbnail, minding its own business.

"Becky, that's ridiculous. You're a grown woman (19), and it's only an eensy, weensy spider. Why don't you get rid of it?"

She paled, and I noticed the gooseflesh rise on her arms. "Oh, no—I couldn't. Please, Mom, will you do it?"

I didn't understand her fear of such a small, harmless spider, but rather than lecture her on the basics of courage, I took care of the little fellow by shoving him into a jar and depositing him outside in the garden.

I shouldn't judge Becky so harshly. I've felt fear, too, over things that to other people may be trifles.

I remember my apprehension as I started out to an unfamiliar city where I was to speak. Driving isn't my favorite recreation anyway, and to drive three hours on a busy California freeway scared me. What if I should get lost? What if I took the wrong turnoff? What if I had an accident? What if I were late for the meeting and couldn't share my testimony about the power of God?

Suddenly those little nagging fears looked like that tiny, garden-variety spider. I had studied my map and knew where to turn off. I had given myself plenty of time for an early arrival. I had committed myself into the hands of an almighty, loving heavenly Father. I was His concern. The fears (which usually never happen anyway) were no longer a threat to my peace.

I found that the best way to deal with little fears (or giant ones) is to put them in their proper place—in the garden of God's sovereign will.

"Why are you fearful, O you of little faith?" (Matthew 8:26).

Today's Scripture: Ephesians 5:15-21

LAWNMOWER

The steady growl of my nearly-new lawnmower sputtered a groan and died. I pulled the starter cord. Nothing. I pulled again. And again. How could it die so young? Then I remembered the directions: "Before starting engine, add oil." I'd followed them faithfully all last summer—and broke three finger-nails on that hard-to-reach oil cap. So I quit oiling it.

Yes, that must be the problem. So, removing the cap (and breaking another nail!) I peered into the lit-tle black hole and could see that it was almost empty.

I filled it to the brim. Then I yanked on the cord again—and again—all the while praying that God would restore my lawnmower to its former useful-ness. It coughed up some dust and smoke, then growled to life. All it had needed was a good dose of oil.

Maybe that's what I need too. Oil, in the Bible, sym-bolizes the Holy Spirit, and I find that I'm running low. When I received Christ as my Savior and Lord, the Holy Spirit came into my life to make it His home—and promised never to leave me (Hebrews 13:5a). But I had been so busy working *for* Him that I had neglected coming *to* Him for filling. And since His work can only be done in His power to produce His results, today before I meet my family and before I go out among my fellow workers, I'll commit myself and all I am to Him for filling.

And by His grace, today will be different. I'll not cough, groan, and sputter to a standstill, but with the power of the Holy Spirit I will do the job He has for me today. How about tomorrow? I can go back for another filling tomorrow and the next day and the next.

"Do not be drunk with wine, in which is excess, but be filled with the Spirit" (Ephesians 5:18).

75

BOOKS

Rain pelted the window behind me, adding to my uneasiness. The family, all in bed, had left me alone to finish my latest offering from the book club. I had been snatching quiet moments whenever possible, and when no one else was around. I didn't want them to see what I was reading. It was scary, eery, and demonic. Many of the best-sellers were about the occult, and I was curious.

I love to read, whether the fine print on cereal boxes, the billboards along the highway, or every book that appeals to my own personal taste.

But this was something new to me: the occult, the macabre. I knew my husband wouldn't approve, not only because of the subject matter, but because the dialogue was sprinkled with offensive words. But since the story was exciting, I continued to read.

I'd be appalled if one of my children found the book, so I kept it hidden, only to be brought out when I was alone.

But I didn't feel alone. Was someone looking over my shoulder? I tried to shake off the feeling, but the longer I read, the more prominent the sensation grew.

Words blurred before my eyes—"I will never leave you nor forsake you" (no matter what you do or read). I wasn't alone. I had subjected the Holy Son of God to the ungodly words and thoughts that filled my mind.

76

I closed the book and looked through the other books on my reading table. Some fed the lower nature, some were no more than froth, and some were manipulative and egocentric.

That night I made a decision. The books that I read from now on will be measured by God's standards as found in Philippians 4:8, for it is true that we are what we read. I don't order many books anymore, and my book club may drop me, but I am adding to my Christian growth by reading from God's booklist —and I don't feel uneasy (or ashamed) when I'm reading alone at night.

"Open my eyes, that I may see wondrous things out of Thy law" (Psalm 119:18).

Today's Scripture: Matthew 10:29-31

FLEAS

"What a wonderful Bible conference!" Mimi said to Opa, looking over her notes. "I'm so glad we could come!"

Opa glanced around the rustic room and said, "And we got a nice cabin—even shag carpets."

Scratch-scratch. "I liked what the speaker said about Joseph . . ." Mimi added. Scratch-scratch.

"It should be a great week." Scratch-scratch.

"You know what?" Mimi said, "I feel like something's biting me!"

Scratch. "Me too!" Scratch.

Mimi examined her legs. "Look, I'm covered with tiny red bumps. Do you think I'm getting measles at my age?"

"No. I've got them too."

The next morning more bumps had appeared on their arms and necks.

"You know," Mimi said between scratches, "I think these are flea bites."

"How could that be?"

"I'll bet whoever rented this cabin last week had a dog, and the fleas are in that shag carpet . . . and on us!"

What had started as a long-desired vacation ended abruptly as a short-term irritation. They left the next day. And all they remember of the Bible conference is the fleas.

"Isn't it usually the little things of life that get us down? A little worry. A thoughtless word. An icy glance. And we give it our complete attention, unaware of the blessings that surround us. Leaving the cabin solved my parents' immediate problem, but the fleas were still in there, waiting to attack the next week's vacationers.

We don't need to run from little annoyances today, and let's not scratch at them all day either. By bringing our problems to the Lord, no matter how small, we can be relieved.

A woman challenged the minister after his message about God's concern over every detail of our lives. "it's presumptuous to think that God wants to hear about our little problems," she said.

His wise answer was, "But, lady, can you tell me what things are big to God?"

". . . casting all your care upon him, for he cares for you" (1 Peter 5:7).

Today's Scripture: Psalm 119:105-112

BANKS

Barby held the pig in her hand, thrust the knife blade into its back, and began to shake it vigorously.

"Sacrificing a pig?" I asked. "How gross!"

She continued to operate on the piggybank as coins, large and small, dropped through the slot and onto the table.

"I thought you were saving your money for a rainy day," I said, gesturing toward the sun's rays streaming through the kitchen window.

"It is a rainy day to me. Today is the last day to get my order in for a yearbook." She looked at the pile of money before her. "Sure hope I have enough!"

The piggybank lay on its side, still smiling, but considerably lighter as Barby counted out the needed five-dollar down payment. He had served his purpose—and saved the day.

Throughout our house is a veritable menagerie of banks. A frog sits glassy-eyed on the bookcase, pennies falling from its mouth. An owl, a dog, and a gray cat hold small, rainy-day treasures like dark clouds awaiting the wind.

Each of us also carries about in our bodies a heart-shaped bank. We store all kinds of special thoughts and dreams to be taken out at a later date and enjoyed.

I'm thankful for these God-given banks of memories—especially on the rainy days that come to all of us. And as I use these stored provisions, I see how important it is to lay aside more than just the pennies and nickels of life. Good memories of good times alone cannot sustain. I find that I need a sound investment, a standard of exchange, that doesn't fluctuate with the changing times. "The law of Thy mouth is better to me than thousands of gold and silver" (Psalm 119:72).

Pain suffered on the hospital bed is eased by God's promise, "Neither shall there be any more pain. . . ." (Revelation 21:4). Sorrow over a loved one's passing lifts as God says, "Precious in the sight of the Lord is the death of His saints" (Psalm 116:15). Loneliness disappears with the remembrance, "I will never leave Thee nor forsake Thee" (Hebrews 13:5).

80

It is the wise person who lays aside for the future. How about banking on this promise? "Thy Word have I hidden in my heart, that I might not sin against Thee" (Psalm 119:11).

❖

Today's Scripture: Matthew 25:14-30

PANS

"Mom, why don't you get rid of this ugly old skillet?" my daughter asked one day while putting away the pots and pans. "You have these new nonstick ones, and they're so much prettier."

I took the pan from her hands and turned it over. It sure wasn't much to look at. It was kind of crusty on the bottom, and it was so heavy—nothing at all like my new "Don't-open-till-Christmas" pans.

That cast-iron skillet was one of our first wedding presents. It wasn't even very pretty then. But I liked the way it cooked. I could simmer a spaghetti sauce in it all day without worrying that it would burn. I could fill it with eggs, each one frying to a perfect doneness, and they wouldn't stick. No, I couldn't get rid of that old pan. It wasn't showy, but it was serviceable. And whenever I wanted to be sure of getting a a job done well, I'd choose my cast-iron skillet over the new ones any day.

I wonder if God chooses His servants in the same way. There are those who are attractive, and bubbling with enthusiasm when the need for a job comes up. They will do it, they say, and probably better than anyone else. So off they go.

The first week or two goes quickly. Never has a job been done so well. But as the months go by, the enthusiasm wanes, and the glamor and glitter grow dim. A good start doesn't necessarily determine a good finish. (Remember the hare and the tortoise?)

Then there are those faithful souls who do any job given to them, perhaps not with the flair of their brothers, but with steady perseverance. They keep at it, not expecting the praise of men, but simply performing a task or the glory of God. Which one will God choose to do His work? Which one am I?

"Let us have grace, by which we may serve God acceptably with reverence and godly fear" (Hebrews 12:28b).

82

STUFFED ANIMALS

"65, 66, 67, I have 67 animals!"

"Maybe you should open a toy store," I said to my 12-year-old daughter. "Either that or move out of your bedroom."

Barby has been collecting stuffed animals since she was old enough to squeal and point at teddy bears. When asked what she wants for her birthday and for Christmas, the answer is always the same—stuffed animals. She loves them and treats them like living animals.

As I opened her closet the other day, there they sat looking straight ahead (rows and rows of them), still and lifeless. They reminded me of a group of women I spoke to last week!

Most of the time I find audiences receptive and warm. Even if there are a few who look like they left their thoughts at home, I can usually spot some in a crowd who are with me. I imagine that most speakers look for the responsive hearers and make eye contact with them from time to time. But the group I stood before last week had all the life of Barby's stuffed animals, except that I think her kangaroo has a warmer smile!

Before me was a roomful of glassy eyes with "noncommittal" written on their foreheads. These were church women—a missionary group. Somehow we just never seemed to get together. I left feeling slightly deflated, but asked God to warm their hearts (and mine) and have His way in our lives.

That experience made me wonder what kind of listener I am. Does my pastor see a "stuffed animal" as he looks at my face on Sunday morning? Do I wear

my "teddy bear" expression when a visiting missionary shares his testimony? If I can listen to a speaker with the idea that we two are alone in the room, my attention will be evident. And if I could visualize my Lord speaking through His Word (because He really does so, you know), I'd certainly sit up and take notice.

How about you?

"Truly I say to you, 'Many prophets and righteous men have desired to see those things which you see, and have not seen them, and to hear those things which you hear, and have not heard them" (Matthew 13:17).

Today's Scripture: Ephesians 6:10-18

TOOLS

"Just wait and see, Mommy," my six-year-old nature boy called over his shoulder. "I'm gonna earn some real money."

I watched him go down the shaded front steps into the blistering hot rays of the Big Valley sun.

"Well, don't be gone long, and stay in the neighborhood," I reminded him. "It's too hot to be outside."

I quickly shut the front door, before the cool air could escape, and watched through the window as an enthusiastic, brown-eyed boy skipped down the street, a box in one hand and a rusty saw blade in the other. What on earth did he have in mind?

An hour later, a sweaty little boy shuffled into the room dragging the empty box and saw. "Didn't you earn any money?" I asked, dabbing at his face with a cool rag.

"No," he said, a big tear oozing from under long, dark lashes, "nobody wanted their lawn cut!"

He had plenty of enthusiasm and even prospective customers, but he didn't have the right tools.

How often do we start a project with the wrong tools? I wouldn't think of painting a wall without paint or writing a book without paper, yet I must admit I've tried to witness about Jesus Christ without the Bible or a working knowledge of God's Word. My experience and enthusiasm isn't enough; it's the Word of God that cuts away the weeds of unbelief.

The work of witnessing may some days be unfruitful, and our spirits droop, but the harvest is ripe and we have the proper tools, so let's be about our Father's business today, armed with enthusiasm and the Word of God.

"Study to show yourself approved unto God, a workman who does not need to be ashamed, rightly dividing the Word of truth" (2 Timothy 2:15).

SUN TEA

Every morning last summer I watched my neighbor set a large jar of clear water on her front sidewalk. There it sat all day, the hot rays of the sun beating down on it. By late afternoon the clear liquid had become a golden brown, and I had become a curious onlooker. As a rule I mind my own business, but. . . .

"Oh, hi, Sharon. May I borrow a cup of sugar?" I glanced over my shoulder at the jar. Maybe when she disappeared into her kitchen I could get a better look.

"Sure, come on in." She walked toward the jar. "I'll give you a glass of tea."

"That's tea?" I blurted.

"Yes. Haven't you ever made 'sun tea'?"

She explained that the hot sun heating the water slowly was what brought out the full rich flavor of the tea.

She was right! It was delicious, and I could hardly wait to try it for myself. So every day throughout the rest of the summer my jar of clear liquid joined hers in the sunshine to be brewed into a cool, satisfying drink. Some days weren't hot enough to draw the entire richness out of the tea bags, and some days I set it out too late. It needed a full day in the hot sun to bring out the maximum richness.

Sun tea reminds me of a life warmed by the Sun of God. I've met some of God's children whose lives are

87

so saturated with His love that being in their presence is a satisfying experience. They tell of trials and testings that, at the time, were almost too "hot" to bear. But they patiently endured—and it shows.

It's important that we trust the wisdom and love of our heavenly Father as His Son shines upon our lives. He knows just how much heat we need to bring out the full flavor of a Christ-controlled life.

What are your circumstances today? Trust God through them. Nothing just "happens" in the life of a Christian. God knows where you are and what you're going through. Let Him bring out the sweetness in your life that can come only through the steady warmth of the Son of God.

"No temptation has overtaken you but such as is common to man, but God is faithful, who will not allow you to be tempted above what you are able" (1 Corinthians 10:13a).

Today's Scripture: Daniel 5:25-31

SCALES

As I read the Bible story of Belshazzar, king of Babylon, where God said, "Thou art weighed in the balances and art found wanting," I feel a slight twinge of envy. Whenever I step on the scales, I never lack anything except the evidence of self-discipline! But I'd rather meet the confrontation of excess poundage on my bathroom scale than those solemn words of God!

Belshazzar was lacking. Although he was king of the world's richest empire, surrounded by worshipful subjects in a palace filled with the wealth of his conquests, God said he was lacking.

I used to think at the Judgment, God would weigh my good works against my bad, and somehow I'd make it into heaven. But that's not His system of measure. My life will be balanced against the Word of God.

What place does Jesus Christ hold in my life today?

Have I wasted precious hours in self-glorification?

What is the motive behind my actions?

Are my works inspired and carried out by the Holy Spirit for the glory of God?

As a compulsive eater and dieter, I get on the bathroom scales regularly to keep myself in check, and I must be just as diligent in weighing my spiritual growth on the Word of God.

By faithfully weight-watching, we may never hear those awesome words that destroyed Belshazzar and his kingdom in one night: "Thou art weighed in the balances and art found wanting."

"Let patience have its perfect work, that you may be perfect and complete, lacking nothing" (James 1:4).

BISCUITS

We hadn't had homemade biscuits for quite awhile, but I was sure I remembered the recipe.

"Let's see, take two cups of flour, about one teaspoon of salt, one-fourth cup of sugar, and three teaspoons of hmm—oh, yes, baking soda. To that I add one-half cup of shortening, cut it in, then mix with approximately three-fourths cup of milk."

I cut the buscuits into neat little circles and baked at 450° for 10 minutes. They smelled delicious, and the family eagerly gathered around the breakfast table for bacon, eggs, and homemade biscuits.

As I took them out, I could feel my face fall as flat as those biscuits. They looked like bricks. They even *tasted* like bricks. That recipe had never failed before. What had I done wrong?

I pulled out my cookbook and quickly ran my finger down the list of ingredients. Oops! There it was. I should have used baking *powder*, not baking *soda*. I thought I knew it all, yet one wrong ingredient ruined the whole batch. I'll remember next time.

I've had the same disastrous results in more important matters than biscuits—my service for the Lord. In depending on past experiences, I've often forgotten the reason for success was that all-important ingredient, the life-giving Spirit of God. Without dependence on His power, my service was as flat and

90

tasteless as those biscuits. If I want God's "yes-work," I can't rely on my "guess-work" when it comes to serving God.

Will I ever learn? I mean really learn to depend on His strength instead of on my own weakness? I will when I finally get my eyes off self and what others think of me, and turn my attention to Jesus Christ and pleasing Him. Only then will my service be satisfying to the hungry. Only then will I "rise" to the occasion.

"Abide in Me, and I in you. As the branch cannot bear fruit of itself, except it abide in the vine, no more can you, unless you abide in Me" (John 15:4).

Today's Scripture: 1 Corinthians 4:3-5

BAND-AIDS

"What on earth happened to you?" I asked in amazement. My little girl had come into the kitchen after a long quiet time in the bathroom, her face covered with Band-Aids.

91

"I had a 'owie,' Mommy," she said, peering out from behind a drooping bandage. "I wanted to be sure I covered it good, so I won't get any germs," she added, patting the bandages lovingly.

"Hmm, looks like you've been in a car accident. Where's the cut?"

Shrugging her shoulders, she said, "Somewhere under here. Sure feels better now."

Her idea of the perfect remedy was little strips of tape and gauze covering her "owie."

Sometimes I try to cover up my own hurts, too. I put on a brave face. I set my lips in a forced smile. I go about my business. But the hurt doesn't heal. It needs more than a covering. It needs proper diagnosis and treatment.

"Father, I have sinned." (Why are those words so hard to utter?) "Left to myself I am nothing. I deserve your judgment, but Christ took it for me. Thank You for Your forgiveness and cleansing, and now help me to make things right with my brother (husband, mother, son, etc.)."

As the blood of Jesus Christ cleanses me, peace and joy cover the hurt, and I'm ready once more to meet the day.

Band-Aids are good for superficial cuts, but utterly fail in treating a severed limb; and self-doctoring can never reach deep enough to treat the sin in my nature. Only the cross can penetrate so deeply.

"He was wounded for our transgressions, He was bruised for our iniquities; the chastisement for our peace was upon Him, and with His stripes we are healed" (Isaiah 53:5).

Today's Scripture: Matthew 7:24-29

HOME PERMANENT

"Are you sure it's all right to leave it on this long?" Christy asked, patting her towel-covered head.

"Don't worry about it, Honey. I've given myself dozens of home-permanents, and I've never had a bad one."

She smiled and sat back in her chair. "You're right. I won't worry. But you know how fine my hair is."

Hmm. Maybe she should be worried. Her hair was awfully fine—and I hadn't even read the directions. I probably should have used the "gentle" permanent instead of the "super" one on her hair.

"Maybe we'd better unroll your curlers now," I said.

As Christy leaned over the kitchen sink, I unwound the rollers and held my breath.

"How does it look, Mom? Mom, answer me!"

"Well. . . ."

I followed her down the hall to the bathroom, where she stood staring in the mirror. "Oh, no! Oh, no!"

She looked just like Little Orphan Annie, with her fuzzy blonde hair and her big round eyes staring blankly at the mirror. Her voice came out in little spurts—"Straightener. We can put some straightener on it."

It took months for her once-lovely hair to return to normal, and although she forgave me for not follow-

93

ing directions, I doubt if she'll ever ask me to do her hair again.

How foolish not to follow the instructions that come with home-permanents—or any other do-it-yourself project. We even get "operation manuals" with our dishwashers, garbage disposals, and microwave ovens. And we should read them.

Are we as negligent about daily reading and following "God's Instructions for Life"? The Bible is accessible to most people of the world. It has been translated and printed in thousands of languages and dialects, yet the human race is in trouble. There are wars and rumors of wars. There is strife and hatred. We are on the brink of destroying ourselves. Could it be because we have failed to read and follow the directions?

"Blessed is he who reads and they who hear the words of this prophecy, and keep those things which are written in it: for the time is near" (Revelation 1:3).

Today's Scripture: John 3:14-21

PAPER BAG

"Just hold the paper bag over your mouth, blow out all your breath, twist up the end, and throw the bag away."

The directions were simple enough, and the newspaper reported that thousands of bags were used regularly by well-known and influential people—to get rid of guilt.

Disposable guilt bags, they're called. Blow it out and throw it away. At least, say the users, they are cheaper than years of on-couch therapy by psychiatrists (and just as effective).

If there were a cheap way to rid ourselves of guilt,

God would have provided it. But there is no easy way out. Man is guilty: guilty of unbelief, disobedience, and rebellion. But God has provided a way out, a way that was neither simple nor easy. It was at great cost, greater than the 40-dollar-an-hour fee charged by "shrinks," yet free to those willing to avail themselves.

God Himself took the form of a Man and lived a perfect, sinless life in a little country called Palestine. There He presented Himself a Sacrifice for man's sin. He poured out His life's blood on Calvary's cross, bearing the guilt of every man, woman, and child ever to walk the earth. And then to prove the validity of His sacrifice, He rose from the dead and ascended back into heaven.

So why waste the time, money, and self-effort to get rid of guilt when all it takes is a look of faith at the Savior? Just a sincere look, and the guilt is gone. "The burdens are lifted at Calvary."

You don't need to carry the guilt of harsh-words-better-left-unspoken or I-wish-I-hadn't-done-that.

Jesus is waiting, His nail-pierced hands outstretched in love. Give Him your guilt, and let Him give you His peace. What a trade!

"Look to me and be saved, all the ends of the earth, for I am God, and there is none else" (Isaiah 45:22).

WASHDAY

Before the dawning of the new age—of automatic clothes dryers—washday was no breeze. One day, after stripping all the beds, washing the sheets, carrying the heavy basket to the line, and pinning up the blue-white muslin to dry, I was pooped!

I flopped down in a chair and sighed to Kathy (then about five years old), "Oh, how I dread having to bring them all back in and make the beds!"

"But, Mommy, that's the best part. We even sing about it in Sunday school."

"We do?" I strained my brain trying to think of the hymn about washday. "Whiter than snow?" I guessed.

"No. Remember the song that says, 'We will come rejoicing, bringing in the *sheets*'?"

Oh, out of the mouth of babes! Ever after that day, my laundry has had a holy glow about it.

Children are so logical. Words carry pictures to their bright, inquiring minds. Kathy had no knowledge of "sheaves," but she did understand "sheets," so her interpretation of Biblical truth was slightly off-center.

The same was true of Barby when she asked about the songleader: "Mommy, why does that man want oil in his lap?"

I've often wondered why my witnessing isn't more

effective. Could it be that the listener doesn't understand my words? "Have you been born again?" Huh?

"There is salvation in none other."

"Redemption, justification, reconciliation, propitiation." These are great words that portray beautiful truths to those taught in Scripture, but to my next-door neighbor and the grocery clerk, my "Christianese" sounds like gobbledygook!

I need to learn this lesson: when sharing eternal truths, I must speak clearly and in a language suitable to the hearers. Jesus spoke simply enough for a child and profoundly enough for a priest, and as I study His methods in the Gospel accounts and apply them, I may just begin to see others stepping into the kingdom of God.

"My speech and my preaching was not with enticing words of man's wisdom, but in demonstration of the Spirit and of power" (1 Corinthians 2:4).

Today's Scripture: 1 Corinthians 12:8-18

GIFTS

"Daddy's home! Daddy's home!" Ten little feet thundered past me toward the front door to meet Daddy as he returned from a business trip. My feelings were a mixture of joy (at seeing the love of my life) and relief (at sharing the responsibility of five children, ages ten to two).

After hugging and kissing all of us, Daddy reached into his bag and pulled out gifts for everyone.

Paper and ribbon flew around the room amid squeals of pleasure. "Oh, thank you, Daddy! See, I got a new car!"

"Look at mine! Thanks, Daddy. How'd you know I wanted a book about stars?"

"Oh, Mommy, look what Daddy brought me—china dishes."

"See, I got a bottle for my dolly."

Content to be home, Daddy sat back in his chair, then suddenly leaned forward and picked up the baby. "What's the matter, Sweetie? Why are you crying?"

"Daddy not bring me present," she sniffed.

"Yes, I did. Where is it? You were so busy looking at the other children's that you must have mislaid it."

Sure enough, there it was, hidden under gift paper and ribbon: just the perfect gift for a two-year-old—a cuddly stuffed kitten. She held it closely to her face and with shining eyes said, "Thank you, Daddy."

As I watched my family, I thought of our heavenly Father, who gives good gifts to all His children. He knows exactly which gift is best for each one, but sometimes we become so occupied with looking at the gifts He has given *others* that we ignore His gift to us. The Bible teaches that God gives the gifts of the Spirit to His children as it pleases *Him*. We're not to plead with Him for certain gifts or to covet other people's gifts.

My husband brought me a gift, too, but my primary interest was in him. *He* was what I wanted—just to be with him, to hear his voice, to rest in his presence.

Where are we today in God's family? Still childishly begging for gifts? Let's leave the gift-giving to Him, and instead concentrate on loving and seeking the Giver rather than the gift. "All these works that one Spirit, dividing to every man individually as He wills" (1 Corinthians 12:11).

Today's Scripture: 1 Corinthians 2:9-12

GLASSES

When I could no longer hold a book far enough away to see the print clearly, I admitted I needed glasses and went for an eye examination.

"You're definitely farsighted," the doctor said, "but since you've never worn glasses before, I don't recommend bifocals." (Great! Maybe no one will know I'm over 40!)

Since now I have reading glasses, and it's a relief to read a book without having to stand across the room, but now (with glasses on) I can't even see across the room. I'm constantly putting them off and on. It's impossible to read while watching TV anymore unless I cock my glasses halfway down my nose and peer over the top. Maybe I should have gone the bifocal route.

I know my spiritual glasses should be bifocals. It's not enough to see present needs excluding the future, and vice versa. This may be a problem you share.

When our attention is focused solely on today's wants and needs, we become self-centered and demanding, and we lose sight of the future—and others.

I can be so involved in my own family that I neglect world issues, or so "otherworldly" that I forget my own family and neighbors.

How can I have a clear, God-given vision of my responsibilities? By setting goals, nearsighted and farsighted, and writing them down.

What must be done today? Who can I help today? How can I grow today? What does God want to teach me today?

How about tomorrow, next month, five years from now? As I seriously consider each question and write down my goals, I begin to see clearly.

No one ever accomplished anything without a goal. Even God Himself looked down through the ages, planned for a Redeemer, and predestined a people for Himself.

Do you have a goal for today? For 10 years from now? Let's polish up our bifocals so we can see where we're going.

"We look not at the things which are seen, but at the things which are not seen; for the things which are seen are temporal, but the things which are not seen are eternal" (2 Corinthians 4:18).

Today's Scripture: Matthew 10:26-30

THROW RUG

"Oh, I see you got a new throw rug today," said my husband as he came through the kitchen door.

I kissed him a "Welcome home," and chirped, "Yes, do you like it? Doesn't it look nice between the stove and the sink?" I hoped he wouldn't ask why I bought it.

We have a narrow, galley-type kitchen, and the 4' x 6' rug fit the area perfectly—and it did add a nice homey touch. Besides, it covered up the eaten-away-wax splotch left by spilled cleaning solution. I tried and tried to get that extra-clean spot to blend with the old wax buildup, but the longer I worked the worse it looked. I had a choice—either strip the entire floor of wax (an all-day job on my hands and knees) or else cover the spot with a rug.

As I finished setting the dinner table, I heard my husband come into the kitchen and mumble, "Hmm, maybe the rug should be moved down a bit. . . ." The mumble became a roar: "Hey, what's this?"

I'd been found out! My spot had grown into a monster —with a pointing finger. I felt guilty for not being honest about my accident with the cleaner, and guilty for trying to cover it up. But when I started to lie about how the cat knocked over the bottle, I decided to 'fess up.'

We had a good laugh and decided the rug *did* look nice there (and we hope no one peeks under our throw rug!).

I've tried covering up sins in my life, too. Sometimes I just don't want to take the time to confess the sin to the Lord and receive His cleansing. Sometimes I think, "Oh, it's just a little sin; surely God won't notice." And sometimes I don't even recognize it when I sin. I just throw a rug over it, thinking that if I don't see it anymore, it probably isn't there.

But it is, and sooner or later it must be dealt with. Why not face up to my sins today? Pull off the throw rugs of self-righteousness and allow the cleansing blood of Christ to lift the stain of guilt. With nothing hidden, I can live my life before God and my fellow-man fearlessly and confidently. I won't have to worry about the rug being lifted and hearing those words, "Hey, what's this?"

"There is nothing covered that shall not be revealed, and nothing hidden that shall not be known" (Matthew 10:26).

❖

Today's Scripture: Luke 12:15-21

CREDIT CARDS

At a luncheon I recently attended, a prize was offered to the woman with the most credit cards in her purse. After a few minutes of scrambling and counting, several voices called out. "I have *five*." "I have *seven*." "I win. I have *ten*."

But those women were only beginners when it came to "plastic money." The winner had 17 credit cards at her disposal!

"There's an example of a trusting husband," said the woman on my left.

"Or a bankrupt one," added the woman on my right.

This is the day of the credit card. We buy now and pay later. Convenience is only one of its attributes. We don't have to carry large quantities of money; we have a computerized record of our spending; and when towels go on sale a week early, we don't have to wait for end-of-the-month paydays.

But as with most privileges of life, there is also a responsibility—a day of reckoning. How easy it is to flip out a credit card to satisfy the desire of the minute, and how hard it is to make those high interest payments over the next year! If we exercise our credit buying with one eye on the sure-to-come bills, we will be wise stewards of our "Lucite lucre."

Remember the story Jesus told of the farmer who had so much material wealth that he decided to build bigger and better barns and get all he could out of life? He forgot about the future reckoning with God and lived only to "eat, drink, and be merry." But God had a surprise for him: no more credit. It was time to pay up: "This night your soul shall be required of you" (Luke 12:20).

Many of us live like we use our credit cards. If we want it, we get it. But God expects us to use wisely all that He has entrusted to us—our money, our talents, our time, and, above all, our souls. We need to be alert to the subtlety. We can't take advantage of God's grace like an ill-used credit card and not expect those solemn words, "This night your soul shall be required of you."

Let's be a credit to Jesus by giving the Master charge!

❖

Today's Scripture: Song of Solomon 4:10-15

LEFTOVERS

After hearing what my friend, Betty, had done with her leftovers, I decided to look into my refrigerator to see if I could come up with a comparable gourmet dish. I gathered up the various sizes and shapes of plastic containers, my mouth watering at the remembrance of Betty's culinary efforts.

My eyes squinted involuntarily as I lifted the first lid. The odor was unfamiliar and the green glob inside couldn't have graced our table within the past month!

I was more cautious as I raised the second lid. Ah, a few chunks of last Sunday's pot roast. That may be a start. I found a shriveled potato and a bowl of something brown and crackly that had possibly been gravy. Maybe if I added a little water. . . .

There was also a quarter-cup of corn, a bowl of half-eaten pudding, a peanut butter sandwich minus one bite, and a container of cranberry sauce—not enough to make a gourmet meal, no matter how imaginative I might be.

It seems there's never enough left over to be worthwhile, yet I hate throwing out those small portions left in the vegetable bowls.

It's wise to be frugal and not wasteful, but there are some things that are not palatable if they are left over, especially after the passing of time.

I've been guilty of storing away God's blessings, too, thinking they may come in handy someday when I don't have the time or inclination to seek His face for a fresh blessing. Just as the manna which was provided for the children of Israel in the wilderness spoiled if kept overnight, so the blessing of God loses its satisfying freshness if hoarded. Have you ever given a leftover testimony or heard a leftover sermon? How dull and dry. How unpalatable.

Let's take time today to feed on God's Word, expecting Him to satisfy us with His goodness. God wants to meet us in the present moment. He lives. And because He lives, I too may live as I daily feast at His table.

"I sat down under his shadow with great delight, and his fruit was sweet to my taste. He brought me to the banqueting house, and his banner over me was love" (Song of Solomon 2:3b,4).

MY LIST

"Where's my list?" I called through the house. "It was right here on the coffee table."

What a mess! I'd be glad when the holidays were over and the kids were back in school. Such confusion!

It had been a day of blocking, tackling, and punting, with my husband cheering and grumbling from his corner chair. What a way to start a new year!

"Where's my list?" I asked again.

My husband tore his eyes away from the flower-covered floats and high-stepping majorettes. "Why are you making such a fuss over an old list?"

"It's not just any old list—it's my New Year's resolutions."

"Oh, I'm sorry, Mom," my daughter interrupted, "I think I threw it away. It just looked like a bunch of words on paper. I didn't know it was important."

Oh, well. Every year I make the same resolutions, and I forget them before the week is over. I guess they were just empty words on paper.

Some people think of the Bible that way too. They mentally dismiss its words as easily as a list of New Year's resolutions. But God's Word is eternally true. We can count on His promises to us every day—all year.

Our days may consist of ordinary events in ordinary places among ordinary things, but although

108

these things may be "ordinary," we have an extra-ordinary God. And we can experience His life fully and bountifully even in our ordinary circumstances. That's a promise. So let's take one day at a time, greeting it with the expectancy of opening a beautiful gift from a loved one. For so it is.

> Each new day so fresh and clean
> Comes as a gift from Thee.
> So Lord, I quickly gave it back
> That Thou canst keep for me.

"His compassions fail not; they are new every morning, great is Thy faithfulness" (Lamentations 3:22,23).

Today's Scripture: John 15:1-6

ROOTS

I'll never write an epic novel, but I've sure learned something about my roots this week. Oh, they're not my family roots—just plain old plant roots.

I mentioned before how much I love house plants—

and how pitiful they are at my house. Fortunately, my husband has taken them over, and they seem to be doing better. However, there was this one Boston Fern that was my favorite, that I wanted to continue nourishing and loving. After all, hadn't I kept it alive for more than six months? This was a new all-time high for me!

There it sat in its little pot, spilling its long, feather-like fronds over the edges. I was so proud. Then it happened. The foliage began curling up, turning brown, and falling off! Since Barby was studying botany, I asked, "Do you have any idea what's wrong with this plant?"

"It may be rootbound. See, look at this." She lifted the entire plant out, its rootball a mass of twisted, stunted strings. It had apparently choked itself to death.

Physically speaking, it is impossible to choke ourselves to death, but we can do it spiritually. Recently, I was involved in a situation in which I responded with bitterness. I didn't even want to pray about it. First Thessalonians 5:18, "In *everything* give thanks, for this is the will of God in Christ Jesus concerning you," rubbed against the raw edges of my conscience. This was one of those "everythings," but the praise wouldn't come. I was defeated and withering.

Then I thought of my Boston Fern. Its bound-up roots had choked the life out of it, and the root of bitterness spoken of in Hebrews 12:15 was choking the life out of me. I bowed before the Lord and asked Him to pull out that root (I couldn't do it myself), and He did!

When that bitterness was removed, I found the praise of God once more flowing through my lips. And get this! God resolved the entire problem in just a few short weeks. Praise God!

If you're dying on the vine today, maybe your roots are in trouble. Let the Gardener of heaven do a little cultivating in your spirit, and you'll find a fresh new awareness of His life flowing through you. ". . . lest any root of bitterness spring up and trouble you" (Hebrews 12:15b).

❖

Today's Scripture: Matthew 23:25-28

PLUMBER'S HELPER

I gripped the long handle of the oversized suction cup and shifted my weight forward—then pulled up with all my might. Down. Up. Down. Up. What a plugged drain! The only water that escaped the sink was on the floor—and me. Two bottles of liquid drain cleaner hadn't moved the obstruction, and all my puffing and panting had done nothing to relieve the problem. I'd have to call the plumber.

He arrived the first thing next morning—cool, clean, and confident. He left three hours later—dripping, dirty, and defeated (after calling an older, more experienced man). Finally we heard that beautiful sound, "S-l-u-r-p, glug, glug." At last, with the pipes free of collected grease and grime, the stagnant water drained out of the sink as fresh, clean water splashed in.

Before he left, I hemmed and hawed around, trying to think of some way to share Christ with him. Nothing seemed right, so I muttered something like, "A—a—do you go to church?"

"No," he said as he handed me the bill and walked through the door.

Well, I tried. Or did I? Why was it so hard to speak out for Christ? I had the Word of God, the Water of Life—but it just wouldn't flow.

My pipes were stopped up! Accumulated bits of indifference and apathy had been hardened by unconfessed sin. The garbage of worldliness and self-righteousness had blocked the flow of life-cleansing words. I needed a Plumber.

As I confessed my sin and failure to the Lord, He applied the cleansing power of the blood of Christ to my life (as in 1 John 1:9). Once again I was in fellowship with my God, and I was an open channel of His love.

I try to remember now that if I want to be an effective witness for Christ, each day's accumulation of this world's dirt must be confessed and cleansed.

"You blind Pharisees, first cleanse what is within the cup and platter, so that the outside of them may be clean also" (Matthew 23:26).

❖

Today's Scripture: Psalm 127:3-5

BABY AND I

It's dusk. Birds twitter their good nights as they settle into their nests. The house is empty except for my baby and me. We curl up together on the couch; her soft blonde hair brushes against my face. Her body fits into the curve of my arm. We are quiet. I relish the joy of the moment. I guess I thought there would always be babies, but now even this one, the last of my brood, will one day soon be too big to cuddle.

How I've enjoyed her! We all have. She arrived in our family when the oldest was fifteen and the youngest was six. She was mothered and loved by three "fathers" and four "mothers" (including Daddy and me). Since she was so much younger than the other children, she was no threat to them and didn't know the meaning of sibling rivalry. She simply loved. I believe she is a special gift from God, and I know He has great plans for her.

As she nestles here in my arms, I remember another day many years ago when I wrote a poem about her. Maybe my memories of her babyhood will bring back some memories to you, too.

> We stand at the kitchen sink,
> washing dishes and laughing,
> making silly faces—
> my baby and I.
>
> We lie on the floor,
> looking at pictures
> of faraway places—
> my baby and I.
>
> We clasp our hands together,
> running through grass
> with bare feet—
> my baby and I.
>
> We rest our heads on the pillow,
> whispering soft secrets
> till falling asleep—
> my baby and I.

Just as our children are so dear to us, so are we to our heavenly Father. He loves to have us settle down with Him and share our secrets. He loves to have our companionship and dreams. We never grow too big to lean on God.

"Draw near to God, and He will draw near to you" (James 4:8a).

❖

Today's Scripture: Exodus 34:29-35

MASKS

"I wanna be a clown!"

"I'm gonna be a hobo."

"I was a cat last year; I think I'll be a gypsy this year."

Every year about the time the leaves begin to turn various shades of gold and brown, my children (and yours) think about what they will be for Halloween. They love to put on masks and pretend to be something or someone other than themselves. From Donald Duck to the Mummy who walks, they've been almost every character possible over the past 24 years (my oldest son started at the age of four.)

I've had fun thinking up costumes for them to wear, and occasionally I've even dressed myself up to scare the trick-or-treaters who ring my doorbell. But to be honest, I'm glad when that night is over and the masks are off. I prefer those dimply pink faces to scarecrows and Raggedy Anns any day.

God prefers us to be open-faced with Him, too. And so do our friends. I have several masks I keep in reserve for special occasions: the "sure-of-myself" one when I have to lead in a discussion or speak before strangers; the "shy" one to cover up my insecurity in a crowd the "smiley-face" mask for Sunday morning after an argument with my husband; the "gloomy Gus" one when I want sympathy. Then there's the "holier-than-thou" mask reserved to wear around "sinners."

It's time to get rid of all the masks—to be honest with others and with myself. After all, God sees right through my mask and loves me anyway, so why not accept myself as I am and trust God to make me what I should be? No amount of mask-wearing is going to change me; only God can do that.

Moses' face shone after he had been in the mountain with God, and because this phenomenon frightened the people, Moses covered his face with a veil. I heard a preacher project the idea, "What if Moses' face no longer shone, but he continued to wear the veil so the people wouldn't know?"

Suppose I am wearing the mask of a consecrated

Christian, but in reality am dragging one foot in the world? Who's to know?

"The Lord does not see as man sees, for man looks on the outward appearance, but the Lord looks on the heart" (1 Samuel 16:7b).

BLUEPRINTS

"See, here's the entryway, and this is the auditorium."

"Here's the stairway leading to the second floor."

"And look at all those classrooms."

A group of excited people gathered around the blueprints of our new church building. What had been several years of talking, negotiating, and praying was finally taking shape. The blueprints were drawn, and we could now visualize what would soon be our new, more-adequate facilities.

It was important that every detail be shown on the blueprints, or else it would be left out. After the approval of the building committee, work would begin!

I'm sure that as God looked down through the ages and saw the church He had designed, His heart too was filled with joy. He had lived in a tabernacle in the wilderness and a temple in Jerusalem, and one day He would live in the hearts of His own children, "The church of the living God." Groundwork was laid, intricate blueprints were drawn, the price was paid in full—Jesus died once for all, the just for the unjust— and God's temple on earth was begun. It isn't completed yet. Each person who puts his trust in the death and resurrection of Jesus Christ becomes a part of that corporate body, the temple of God. But

118

just as truly, each and every one is *individually* the temple of God.

Why does God need a temple? To reveal Himself to mankind. His perfect revelation of Himself was in the visible Person of His Son, and today he continues to reveal Himself as the Holy Spirit indwells believers.

What a privilege! What a responsibility! As I go about the earth in my body, am I honoring God? Are the places I go, the things I do, the words I speak evidences of the God who lives within me? How can I know what is expected of me as the temple of God? Well, I can study the blueprints and incorporate the details and specifics in my life.

God's Word, the Bible, is His blueprint. He has left nothing out; He has added nothing that shouldn't be built in. Isn't it exciting to look over His blueprints and see how the finished product will be an eternal honor and glory to Him?

"Do you not know that you are the temple of God, and that the Spirit of God dwells in you?" (1 Corinthians 3:16).

Today's Scripture: John 1:1-14

DICTIONARY

Today I bought a new dictionary, and it's really something else! It is *Webster's New Unabridged Dictionary*, with over 2000 pages of words, plus color plates, maps, foreign phrases, and much more. I could spend hours browsing over the pages, learning new words and understanding old ones.

As I hold that weighty volume in my hands, I feel a sense of awe. Think of all the books that can be written using various combinations of words! Imagine the power exercised by governments and demagogues as they gather up certain words and put them together to communicate their thoughts!

Words can be used to bring a people to its feet or send them to their knees. They soothe sorrowing spirits and fire discouraged hearts. What power there is in these letters placed side by side! Words truly communicate ideas.

"Out of the abundance of the heart, the mouth speaks."

In the first chapter of John's Gospel, much is said about the Word. The Word was in the beginning. The Word was with God. The Word was God. The Word was made flesh and lived among us. The Word was Jesus Christ.

Did you ever wonder why Christ is referred to as the Word? He is the outward expression of God. He is that visible, knowable Communicator of the invisible God. How can we know God? By looking at Jesus. He said, "If you've seen Me, you've seen the Father." He also said, "I and the Father are one." Jesus Christ is the exact image of God.

Satan hates this truth more than any other. Look at the cults and false religions. What do they all have in common? They misrepresent the Person of Jesus Christ. They claim that He was merely a good man—a son of God—a god—a way to God.

Jesus Christ claimed to be *God*. He accepted worship as God. The Jews understood His claims and hated Him for it. He could not have been a good man and lied about His relationship with the Father.

If you're in doubt about a religion, don't concern yourself about its teaching of heaven or hell. Don't be led astray by its doctrine of good works. Find out what they believe about *Jesus Christ*. Who is He?

Jesus is the Word. He is God.

"Let this mind be in you, which was also in Christ Jesus, who, being in the form of God, coveted not to be equal with God" (Philippians 2:5-6).

Today's Scripture: Genesis 8:20-22

PERFUME

Do I want to "stay on his mind" or be a "24-hour woman"? I received several different fragrances for Christmas, and I have this *big* decision to make every evening before my husband comes home from work. Should I be "as fresh as all outdoors" or "darkly mysterious"? I glanced at my reflection in the mirror—blue jeans and T-shirt—and decided I'd need more than perfume to change my image.

I dashed into the shower, scrubbed myself with the

soap that "people who like people" use, and slipped into a fresh blouse and skirt. I dabbed a little "brings-out-the-animal-in-him" behind each ear and looked at the clock.

In one hour I had dinner (fried chicken and broccoli) on the table, with flour in my hair and grease on my nose.

"Hmm, Honey," my husband whispered in my ear, "you smell good—like fried chicken!"

Oh, well, they say the way to a man's heart is through his stomach. My perfume didn't bring out the animal in him, but the smell of food did!

Smells, odors, and fragrances do affect the way we feel about others and ourselves. Whether my husband noticed my perfume or not, I knew I was wearing it, and I felt feminine and desirable.

God has given us the gift of smell, and I'm thankful for it. We can smell if something is burning, if it is clean or dirty. And who can resist burying his or her nose in a bright red rose or a new book?

There's a fragrance that pleases God, too.

"Therefore, be followers of God, as dear children, and walk in love, as Christ also has loved us and has given Himself for us as an offering and a sacrifice to God for a sweet-smelling savor" (Ephesians 5:1,2).

The love of Christ that led Him to give up His life as a Sacrifice for our sins is more fragrant to God than the most expensive perfume money can buy. And as we are followers of Him, we too can be a sweet breath in His nostrils.

Let's respond to Christ's love and sacrifice through a total commitment to Him, and give ourselves in love to others.

123

GROCERIES

The grocery shopping is done for another week. Each trip to the market brings higher prices and fewer bags. I almost dread having to make the decisions of what to serve my family. How I'd love a good steak—but the price of beef is astronomical. And which is the better buy among brands of frozen orange juice? The cheaper one is bitter, so it isn't really better. And the bread—the inexpensive brands are airy and full of preservatives. What a difficult choice!

Then I not only have to cart all the food into the kitchen from the car, but I also have to decide on which shelves to use.

I'm ashamed—ashamed of my complaining when I have so much to be thankful for. I have shelves and shelves of food to choose from, a regular paycheck, and a healthy appetite.

I don't have to go out and hunt for food or look for scraps in my neighbor's garbage cans. I've never missed a meal because of lack of food. I've never felt the pain of hunger or malnutrition. And here I am, complaining because I have so much food that I don't know where to store it!

Please forgive me, Lord. Give me the spirit of thankfulness that comes from recognizing Your Presence in my life. All these good things come from You—the abundance, the shelves, the strength to purchase, to cook, to eat.

I sit at the table,
smiling, loving,

124

And think of those who hunger,
crying, dying.
I pray that I may be
thanking, giving.

"Make a joyful noise unto the Lord. . . . Serve the Lord with gladness; come before His Presence with singing. . . . Enter into His gates with thanksgiving, and into His courts with praise. Be thankful to Him, and bless His name, for the Lord is good; His mercy is everlasting, and His truth endures to all generations" (Psalm 100:1,2,4,5).

Today's Scripture: 2 Samuel 22:33-37

PLUGS

Our family had spent a wonderful week in a rented cabin at our favorite mountain resort. Since we were expected to leave the place clean for the next week's inhabitants, each person chose a job and got busy scrubbing, dusting, and vacuum cleaning.

I *thought* my daughter was vacuuming, but I didn't hear the motor running. As I peeked into the living room, bustling with noise and activity, I watched a few minutes as Christy puffed and pushed the nearly-new canister-type vacuum cleaner. "Boy, for a new sweeper, this thing sure doesn't do the job!" she called over her shoulder. I didn't answer, but picked up the dragging cord and followed her around the room.

"Could this have anything to do with it?" I asked, dangling the plug in front of her face.

"Oh, no, you mean it wasn't plugged in?"

No, it wasn't plugged into the source of power, and no matter how new the machine or how diligently she pushed the sweeper, it was useless unless connected.

I've often experienced failure as I witnessed to others and tried to serve the Lord, simply because I wasn't plugged into the Source of power.

His power is always available; just a simple look of faith, an unspoken word of prayer, or a cry for help will supply the connecting link to the power of God.

Power is manifested in many ways. It makes refrigerators cold and stoves hot. A radio transmits sound and a television displays pictures. The fan over the stove sucks in air and the fan in the furnace blows it out. Power operating in the lives of God's children is also seen in diverse ways. One sins, another preaches. One writes, another teaches.

My friend neither teaches or sings; she prays. She prays all night as God touches her heart with the needs of His people.

How does God manifest Himself through you and me? We can plug into His power to-day—*NOW*—before wasting time and energy through unconnected self-effort.

"You shall receive power after the Holy Spirit is come upon you" (Acts 1:8).

MONEY

Money. Who needs it? We all do. We need to pay the rent, buy the food, keep the kids in shoes, put gas in the car, and give Uncle Sam his share. Many of our problems result from not having enough (or perhaps too much) of this substance we call money.

There was once a popular song that proclaimed, "Money is the root of all evil." but God's Word says, "*Love* of money is the root of all evil" (1 Timothy 6:10a). So the questions I ask myself today are: What place does money have in my life? How often do I think about it? What would I do to get it? How would I use it if I had it? Does God's work get a portion of my money?

I once heard of some people who tried to teach their children the proper attitudes toward money by leaving great sums of cash on top of the mantle in the living room.

They believed the accessibility of the money would teach not only good stewardship, but also honesty. They would take only what was needed and record it on a balance sheet. Most of the time the arrangement worked as planned, but occasionally temptation would overcome even the strongest child, and unrecorded coins and bills disappeared from the mantle.

Then came the day of revoking. The guilty party would usually confess and be meted punishment for his breach of trust by a joint agreement of all the family members.

When I heard this story, I was reminded of the Garden of Eden. I suppose those children felt a little

127

like Adam and Eve. The "tree" was there in all its glory, and they weren't supposed to eat of it. They obeyed perfectly as long as their attention was centered on God rather than on their own selfish desires. But once they looked aside, Satan was there to tempt.

Eve *saw* that the tree was good and pleasant to the eyes. She *desired* it. She *took* of the fruit, and not only ate some herself, but gave a piece to Adam, too!

Today if you find yourself tempted to give the wrong emphasis to money or any other "thing," remember the words of James 4:7: "Submit yourselves therefore to God. Resist the devil, and he will flee from you."

Today's Scripture: 2 Corinthians 3:1-6

DOILY

Fran's dinner was superb. I always looked forward to being a guest at her dinner parties. Besides excelling as a gourmet cook, she set an elegant table and managed to invite interesting people. Seated between a neurosurgeon and a magazine publisher, I not only cleaned my plate of chicken kiev, but also ate up every word of my dinner companions. Then came dessert—a cloud-light lemon chiffon set on a lacy paper doily. Beautiful!

The publisher mentioned my writing. (I thought he'd never ask!) As I embarked on my literary interest, while partaking of the luscious offering before me, I was only moderately aware that Fran's piecrust wasn't up to par. *Oh, well, she's only human, after all.*

The publisher didn't seem to be listening, but was instead staring at the table in front of me. Was that a smile playing at the corners of his mouth? (I didn't think it was humorous to receive rejection slips. Why was he laughing at my tale of woe?)

Then I followed his eyes to my plate. Only the outside edges of the doily decorated the dark-blue china. What had happened to the center? As I gasped at the realization of what I'd done, all eyes focused on me.

No wonder the crust tasted like paper. I had eaten the doily!

I learned some lessons from that experience. Don't become so enamored with your own words that you don't know what you're doing. Don't judge the cook —you may be eating the plate! But I think the most important thing I learned that night was not to take myself so seriously. I was embarrassed at first, but when I realized the humor of the situation I was able to laugh along with everyone else.

If we can accept ourselves and our foibles with understanding, patience, and a little humor, we may avoid a bad case of ulcers or loss of self-esteem. After all, we *are* only human. I'm not perfect, but neither was the neurosurgeon or the publisher. You know, after that incident, the party came to life as each person related a similar faux pas from his own past.

"The letter kills, but the Spirit gives life" (2 Corinthians 3:6b).

AFGHAN

"Knit-one-two-three-four. Pearl-one-two-three-oops!" I looked at the row of orange and yellow yarn and wondered if it was ever really going to be an afghan. My neighbor had made one and had written down the directions for me, but after completing about 12 inches, I had my doubts.

This was my first serious knitting project since those many years ago when we all made argyle socks for our boyfriends. Now that was creativity! If I remember correctly, we had used four knitting needles and sometimes as many as eight bobbins dangling from them. I spent most of my time trying to disengage the yellow yarn on the purple bobbin from the purple yarn on the yellow bobbin. Anyway, I think I made four or five pairs of socks (although they weren't exactly pairs).

I gave up the sock business and started a blue sweater in preparation for the birth of my first baby. But when I discovered I'd knitted a two-foot-long sleeve, I was afraid it was an omen of some kind, and I didn't finish it.

Back to the afghan. I hope it is pretty and keeps Kathy warm. If she wants, she can use it for a bathmat. All my children will eventually get a "Mom-made" afghan, like it or not.

It's good to work with your hands, whether it's knitting, sewing, oil painting, or lettering. My next project is a class in calligraphy.

I've heard people say, "Oh, I'm not creative!" I don't believe it. I think God has given everyone a little spark of creativity, and though it may take some of us a long time to find out what we can create, we should keep trying. The first, second, and third efforts are only the beginning. To become proficient in anything, we must continue working at it.

I'm glad we can keep going after initial failures, because I've dropped a lot of stitches in my Christian walk, too. I have given up many times, but God has always been present, pointing out my errors and showing me His way.

"Let us not be weary in well-doing, for in due season we shall reap if we faint not" (Galatians 6:9)

Today's Scripture: Revelation 10:1-6

CLOCKS

There's something about the ticking of a clock that soothes my spirit. It's so steady, so regular. We have several clocks in our home, and we have plans and places for several more. (We've been shopping for a grandfather clock with just the right face and voice.)

The clock radio in the bedroom has no personality whatever. It simply hums until 5:45 A.M., when it awakens us with the poignant words, "Are insects sucking the life out of your plants?"

The kitchen clock is a step up on the scale. It looks like a miniature butcher block and says, "cut-cut—cut-cut."

The family room boasts the newest clock in our house. I'm not sure I can describe it, but I'll try. It's quite heavy and moves down a notched brass bar mounted on a carved wooden plaque. When it reaches the bottom of the bar, you push it back up to the top. The upward motion rewinds it, and it's ready to begin its trip downward again. It hangs next to my chair, and I enjoy its quiet "pluck-pluck" during my early-morning meditations.

The living-room clock is the fanciest. It's made like a carriage lantern—brass with etched glass panels. Little brass balls swing back and forth to the steady "tick-tock."

I had a new thought the other day while thinking about my clocks. *They'll be totally absent in my heavenly home.*

I'm not going to miss them. Just think how it will be without the limitation of time. We'll never say again, "It's time to fix dinner," or "Time to go to bed," or "Can't you kids ever come home on time?"

We'll have a leisurely eternity to worship and serve our God. We won't rush from the reaches of outer space to the throne room and discover that our Father is out to lunch." He will be eternally available, and so will we.

Perhaps just the knowledge of that future freedom releases me to enjoy my clocks and their reminders of passing time until that great and glorious day when ". . . there should be time no longer" (Revelation 10:6b).

PURSE

"Honey, is the checkbook in your purse?"

"Yeah. Go ahead and get it; my hands are wet."

After considerable shuffling, rattling, jingling, and groaning, my husband came into the room, the purse in his hand. "You find it! I've never seen such a mess. Why do you keep all those scraps of paper in your purse?"

I dried my hands and took the bulging bag. Hmmm—I guess it was a little unkempt: three eight-inch-long cash-register receipts: four lists of things to do; expired coupons for Blue Dwarf corn and Limpy paper towels; chewing-gum wrappers; credit card slips; and film and candy papers (why do my kids use my purse for a wastebasket?).

"Here it is," I sighed. "Can't you ever find anything?"

He rolled his eyes heavenward and exited.

I'm afraid my closets and drawers are like my purse—in total disarray. I've tried to change my ways, but you know the old adage about old dogs and new tricks.

It's never too late to change. I may not be able to do it on my own, but God is willing and able to conform me to the image of His Son—and I'm sure He is neat. Just evidence His creation! There's a place for everything, and everything is in its place.

This bad habit can infect other areas of life, too. A mind cluttered with unnecessary trivia produces little in the way of definite solutions. A soul without deliberate, fixed attention on the one true God can be led astray, to its eternal detriment. Here's where goal-setting comes in.

1. Today I will seek God's will through the Bible and prayer.
2. Today I will write those letters.
3. Today I will study that chapter.
4. Today I will clean out my purse, closets, etc.

Let's also straighten out some thinking today—and tomorrow. A task repeated becomes a habit, good or bad.

"I am with you in the Spirit, joying and beholding your order, and the steadfastness of your faith in Christ" (Colossians 2:5b).

Today's Scripture: Phillippians 2:12-14

TYPEWRITER

"Oh, I'll take this one," I said, after typing out the famous words, "Now is the time for all good men to come to the aid of their party."

"Maybe this machine will turn out a best-seller!"

My second-hand electric typewriter had grumbled its last growl and refused to return to the left-hand margin. With every pause it would groan, "Hurry up! Hurry up!" Well, I didn't, so it gave up the ghost.

I brought my new typewriter home and made it

comfortable on a green pad in the center of my typing table. After rolling in fresh paper and situating myself with anticipation, I pushed the "on" switch.

"Hummm," said the typewriter. I was sure the ideas would flow through my fingers to the shiny new keys. Nothing.

"Hummm."

"It's coming, it's coming," I said. I touched the return key and typed the label "Page 1."

"Hummm!"

"Okay, here we go. 'Now is the time for all good men to come to the aid of their party.' " Not much of an opening line!

My fantasies of success *because* of a new typewriter vaporized. I'm learning that success in life (and writing) is not contingent upon possessions. Too often we think, *If only I lived in a different neighborhood, got a new car, or had a beautiful face, my life would be successful.*

Not necessarily. Just as my new typewriter all by itself will never produce a best-seller, neither will a change in circumstances assure me of a prosperous life.

There's no perfect answer to a victorious Christian life, either. There's no perfect church, no perfect preacher, no perfect Christians. But we *do* have a perfect Savior. Let's trust in Him and begin to *work out* what He has *worked into* our lives. It won't just happen by itself.

"Work out your own salvation with fear and trembling, for it is God who works in you to will and to do His good pleasure" (Philippians 2:12b,13).

WALLPAPER

I've just finished my first hanging—of wallpaper, that is—and I'm sure I'll never take a wallpapered room for granted again!

With my husband out of town and Father's Day approaching, I decided to wallpaper the bathroom. So with fern-decorated paper, paste, a brush, and roller, I began what nearly became my Waterloo.

The first strip was a little crooked, but at least it didn't slip off the wall. As I progressed around the room, I noticed that the seams were more horizontal than vertical, so I trimmed the excess paper off when I reached the window. (Maybe the curtains would cover the ragged edges.)

My next obstacle was trying to fit that big slimy gob of wrinkled ferns down behind the toilet. Oh, well, I'd hide the folds and bubbles with a picture. I added a new bathmat set and towels for the finishing touch!

As my tired, dusty husband returned from his backpacking trip and headed for the shower, the children and I cried out, "Happy Father's Day!"

He poked his head out of the bathroom, worked up a weak smile and said, "Wow, thanks, everybody. It sure looks, well, it sure looks—clean!"

Have you ever undertaken a project that you weren't prepared for—and botched it up? I felt that way when I began my family. I didn't know a thing about babies or raising children. But I read a lot of books, talked to other mothers, and experimented on my own.

136

I'm sure I often botched up. I lost my temper when patience was called for. I gave in when consistency was the answer. But I really tried, and I trusted God. I

pray that He will somehow take my mistakes and straighten them out for His glory. I pray that my children will be well-adjusted, contributing

members of the human race. I pray most of all that
they will be, well—clean!

> Holy Father, help me to learn
> As I behold this child
> The lessons that You have for me
> Through Jesus, the Undefiled.
> May I learn quickly to obey,
> As a child must do the same,
> And through this life here on earth
> Bring honor to Your Name.

"Cleanse me from secret faults" (Psalm 19:12).

Today's Scripture: Psalm 127

JEWELS

I love jewels—the way they sparkle and catch the
light. I admire them in the jewelry store, and sometimes I even try on a few rings. Diamonds are my
favorites. They are so clear—like miniature stars
sending out their rays of brilliant color. My neighbor
has a gorgeous stone, and so does my mother. Mine is
nice, too. It's not as large as theirs, but it's nice. It
pleases me.

My husband gave the diamond to me over 30 years
ago. He said it was the reflection of his undying love.
He slipped it on my finger as we sat in a restaurant
holding hands under the table. To me it was the most
beautiful ring I'd ever seen. In all these years it has

continued to sparkle on the third finger of my left hand.

Over the years other jewels have been added as tokens of our love—not diamonds, rubies, or emeralds, but precious children who have brightened our lives with their presence. Oh, I'd be the first to admit they don't always sparkle, and to others they may even seem rough, unpolished, and not jewels at all. But to me they're more valuable than a king's coffer. I'm sure you feel the same about your children.

However, whether we like it or not, they are our adornments. Because they reflect our attitudes and actions, we have a great responsibility to them.

We don't tell them to be kind and thoughtful; we *show* them. We don't teach honesty; we *demonstrate* it. We don't *force* them to worship God; we share our love for Him with them.

How unfair it is when children are born into homes where they are unwanted and unloved! They learn what they see: to be selfish and self-centered. It is hard for such children to grasp the concept of a loving heavenly Father when their idea of a father-figure is a hard, unloving person.

Some days it is difficult to show Christ's love. We are tired, worried, and perhaps ill. We feel upset and unlovely. On those days, as on any other, we may call upon the God of love to minister to our children through us. He is just waiting for our call. He loves our children; He loves us.

"Children are a heritage from the Lord, and the fruit of the womb is His reward" (Psalm 127:3).

CHOCOLATES

A three-pound box of chocolates. That should certainly outlast the Christmas holidays! But it didn't.

"I wonder what kind this is?"

"I think I'll try this one. Ugh!"

"This one looks good."

"If it isn't, try another."

Four people and a three-pound box of candy. What more could you ask for, this side of heaven? With that much candy, no one would notice how many were missing. We managed to gulp down the entire amount in three days—two weeks before Christmas!

The availability of such "forbidden fare" was our downfall. The more we ate, the less satisfied we were, and the more we wanted.

I've had the same problem when I've been overcome with an eating binge. I've stuffed a variety of foodstuffs into that hole in my face until I actually felt nauseous.

Sin creates a similar appetite to those out of fellowship with God. First it's a little sin, perhaps an ungodly thought. Then the thought becomes a desire. The desire, unchecked, leads to outward rebellion against God.

We don't see it that way. We excuse ourselves by saying, *It won't matter if I do it just once. Who's to know. I have my rights.*

But that "little sin" whets the appetite for more *self*-expression, and then follows another sin—and another—until before long we are dull and lethargic toward our relationship with God.

140

Worldiness has won. But are we satisfied? No. Sin never satisfies; it only creates a longing for more—and more.

I believe that God is the only satisfying power in the universe. Even such good endeavors as education, community involvement, and self-giving are not totally fulfilling in themselves.

I'm going to feed upon God's Word today instead of my own desires. I'm going to look to Him for satisfaction—and I know I'll find it.

"They are more desired than gold, than much fine gold; sweeter than honey and the honeycomb" (Psalm 19:10).

Today's Scripture: John 3

ME

We've reached the end of this book, but I hope for both you and me that we have learned to see God in the ordinary things of our lives. I pray that through these devotional thoughts you have become more aware of the Person of God in your home.

We all have highlights—vacations, special friends, holidays—but most of our day-to-day living is neither unusual nor exciting. We have a choice. We may fasten our eyes on our circumstances and lead a humdrum existence, or by faith we may lift our eyes to God and see His lovely hand touching the ordinary and transforming it into the extraordinary.

141

God loves us. He proved it by sending His only Son, Jesus Christ, to die for our sins. Until we acknowledge His claims upon our lives, we are blind to His glorious Presence. We remain dead in our trespasses and sins. A dead man cannot see God.

If you have not yet committed your life, with all its sin (and its self-righteousness) to Jesus Christ, won't you do it today? You'll never be sorry. You will begin to see for yourself the lessons of life that He is teaching.

Here's how you may know God in a personal, vital way.

COME TO JESUS. Jesus said, "I am the Way, the Truth, and the Life; no one comes to the Father except by me" (John 14:6).

BELIEVE ON JESUS.

RECEIVE JESUS. John 1:12 says, "As many as received him, to them gave He power to become the sons of God, even to them that believe on His name."

PRAISE JESUS—You are His! "These things I have written to you who believe on the name of the Son of God, that you may know that you have eternal life, and that you may believe on the name of the Son of God" (1 John 5:13).

Your future eternity, as well as the days ahead, rests upon the decisions you make today. Can you join me in these words?

> Now I've found God's way of life,
> And thought I'm still an average wife,
> Jesus Christ has made me free—
> Free to be extraordinary ME!

I love you.

142